INTERFACE

INTERFACE

Jonathan Fisher

LION EDUCATIONAL

Copyright © 1986 Jonathan Fisher
and copyright holders listed under Acknowledgements

Published by
Lion Publishing plc
Icknield Way, Tring, Herts, England
ISBN 0 7459 1153 6
Albatross Books Pty Ltd
PO Box 320, Sutherland, NSW 2232, Australia
ISBN 0 86760 821 8

First edition 1986

British Library Cataloguing in Publication Data

Fisher, Jonathan
  Interface.
  1. Religions
  I. Title
  291   BL80.2
  ISBN 0-7459-1153-6

Printed and bound in Italy

CONTENTS

HOW TO USE THIS BOOK

This is not an 'easy' book, because the questions it faces are 'hard' questions. When people ask questions such as 'Why am I here?' 'What should I do with my life?' or 'Where am I going?' they are hard questions. They are questions to which answers have been given in religious faith; they are questions which are often explored in literature.

This book starts with extracts from literature which have been written to make people think about such questions and about possible answers. Some questions are more difficult than others. The hardness of some questions, and the difficulty of some of the exercises designed to help us come to grips with them, is recognized in this book. A simple star grading is given with each section. One star (☆) is simpler than the three star (☆☆☆) sections. The sections can be taken in any order and the book used for a term or a year, or in four- to five-week units as part of a wider course.

After you have read the first extract, you will find that there are questions, exercises and, sometimes, further extracts for you to read. You should work through all of the questions with your class or group without writing anything down. Then choose the hardest exercise in a section which you think you can do really well and write out a rough (or draft) answer. Give the draft to a friend and get him or her to check it for you and make any suggestions; do the same for them. Then get your teacher or group leader to go through what you have written, to make suggestions and eliminate any mistakes. Finally, use the corrected rough copy to make a good copy (a fair copy) which you should hand in to your teacher or group leader. This will be kept or 'banked' for you, together with comments on your work.

When a piece of work has been banked from each of the twelve sections, there will be a permanent record of the best work you can do, which gives a record of your progress.

✡ 1
✡ THE BEGINNINGS
✡ OF RELIGION

Religion is one of the most important things in the world. In a world population of about 5,000 million people there are said to be something like 1,000 million Christians, 500 million Muslims, 500 million Hindus, 200 million Buddhists, twelve million Jews and ten million Sikhs. To take just one example, in the United Kingdom, which many people say has rejected the Christian faith on which so many of its laws, customs, literature and works of art are built, there are many more people in church on a Sunday morning than at all of the sporting events on a Saturday! More generally, there is a lot of evidence to show that it is not religion which people have rejected so much as the places where religion is practised. It has been said that 'People have rejected Churchianity, not Christianity.'

But where did religion come from? When did it all begin?

The Vedas of the Hindu religion are some of the most ancient holy books, and they are so old that it is not even known how they originated, except that they came with the Aryan invaders of India. Several writers have written imaginative accounts of people living near the beginnings of time and they have tried to imagine how religion might have started.

In *The Source*, James Michener tells the story surrounding each find of an archaeological 'dig' in Israel. Among the finds are some flints of about 10,000 BCE, and he tells the story of Ur, a cave-dweller to whom they belonged. Ten thousand BCE was a significant time in the history of the land of Israel. It was the period when men were moving out of caves and into primitive houses; when agriculture began to develop alongside herding. The period of change brought unsettled thoughts about the gods. The new situation demanded a new set of beliefs. Ur's son is thinking about some of the injustices which surround him . . .

James
Michener
The Source

Sitting on a rock beside the grain field, the boy watched the hunters depart, then shared with his mother certain speculations that had troubled him: 'In the wadi we have many birds. The black-headed birds that sing in the evening, and those beautiful things with long bills and blue wings that nest in river banks to catch fish. And the crested larks walking about the field out there, searching for grains. And that swift bird, faster than all the rest . . .' He hesitated. 'The one that eats bees.' He pointed to where a bird somewhat larger than his hand, with long sharp beak, blue body and a profusion of bright colours on its wings and head, darted in and out among the trees. It was a magnificent bird, swooping in lovely arches through the sky, but what concerned Ur's son was not its beauty. 'See! He catches a bee in mid-flight. He takes it to a dead branch. And there he eats it. But watch! He spits out the wings. And this he does all day.'

Now the Family of Ur knew, better than most, that bees were an asset to the wadi, and one of the boy's first memories was of his father coming home, near-blinded with stings, swearing and slapping at his beard, with a hoard of honey which the children of the cave had fought for. The flowers of the area were so diverse in flavour that honey from four different combs might taste like four quite different things. For their sting, bees were respected; but for their song and their honey, they were loved. And to think that a bird as alluring as the bee eater existed solely to feed upon bees raised in the boy's mind a whole new range of questions: How could two things, each so excellent, be in such mortal conflict? How could two desirable aspects of nature be so incompatible?

He asked his mother, 'If a bee does so much good in the wadi and is tormented by an enemy as fatal as the bird . . .' He followed the flight of the dazzling predator and watched as it swooped down upon a bee returning from the flowers and then spit out the wings. It was an ugly incident and he said, 'Is it possible that we also have enemies somewhere in the sky, waiting to pounce on us?' Again he paused, and then put into exact words the problem that had begun to torment his mother: 'Suppose the rain has a spirit of its own? Or the sun? What then with our wheat?'

A second aspect of nature led the boy to an even more difficult question. The cypress, that tall and stately tree which marched along the edges of the open fields serving as a dark pointer to the sky, was a splendid tree in whose narrow body birds loved to nest, and it produced each season a crop of small cones about the size of a thumb tip, remarkable for the fact that each contained nine faces cleverly fitted together to hide the seeds inside. There were never eight faces and never ten, but always nine, ingeniously matched in a manner that could not have happened by accident. Some spirit within the cypress had consciously willed its cone to appear as it did, and if this were true of the tree, why was it not also true of the field in which wheat grew? And of the wheat itself?

The boy sat with his mother in the sunlight pondering these matters when a bee eater flew past, creating brilliance in the sky, then disappearing into the cypress trees which stood like warning sentinels. A tantalizing thought played across the boy's mind, a thought not easy to formulate but one that he could not throw aside. A trio of crested larks marched past, pecking for fallen grains, and after they had disappeared he stared at the cypresses and asked, 'Suppose the spirit that forms the beautiful cone is not within the cypress? Suppose the rain comes or stays away not because of what the rain wants to do . . .' His thoughts were leading him into areas too vague and shadowy for him to explore, and for the moment he dropped the matter, but the fear he had aroused would not go away.

---

1   Write a description or make a drawing to show that you understand the following words and phrases in the extract and in its introduction:

'an archaeological "dig"'
'wadi'
'long bills'
'the cypress . . . serving as a dark pointer to the sky'
'small cones . . . which contained nine faces closely fitted together'

---

2   Write dictionary definitions for the following words, if necessary using a dictionary to help you:

speculations   incompatible
profusion   fatal

asset	ingeniously
hoard	pondering
alluring	sentinels

3

Some scholars believe that when people lived in caves, they believed in a spirit which protected them, often linked to a particular animal. The animal was protected by the clan and rituals were developed which made it possible for the protecting spirit of the animal to help them. It was when people moved out of caves and saw more things happening around them that they began to realise that such an idea of a protecting spirit was not enough to explain all they could see. It is this background which guided James Michener in the writing of his story.

Now read the first four paragraphs of the extract again until you reach, he 'put into exact words the problem which had begun to torment his mother: "Suppose the rain has a spirit of its own? Or the sun? What then with our wheat?" '

3.1 What was he thinking the wheat might have?

3.2 What is the belief called that everything which lives or moves has a spirit?

3.3 What might such a belief lead you to do to the rain, sun or wheat?

3.4 In what ways has his thinking gone further than this, even though he cannot understand all he is thinking?

3.5 Find the meaning of the following terms which describe early forms of religion:

Totemism
Animatism
Animism
Polytheism

Which word would you use to describe the religion of the son of Ur?

4

Write about an experience you have had, or an experience that you have heard or read about which somebody else has had, which could make you think that there is more to life than just material things, and might even lead you to believe in God.

OR:

What things happen in the world which might lead you to disbelieve in God?

When you have done this, you might find it interesting to make a survey of how many people in your class or group have had what they would call 'religious experiences'. If you are interested you could find out more about Dr Edward Robinson's work at the Religious Experience Research Unit at Oxford where data has been collected on many experiences of this kind.

---

5   Read again the sentence, 'His thoughts were leading him into areas too vague and shadowy for him to explore, and for the moment he dropped the matter.'

5.1 Try to write down at least three things which you have thought about and have tried to make sense of, but which you have found too difficult. Explain what you thought about them as far as you can.

5.2 Do you think that there are some things which are beyond the reach of human knowledge, or do you think that, given time, we will one day know everything? Give careful reasons for your answer.

5.3 Find and read the story of the Buddha until he came to 'enlightenment' and record the story in a notebook. When you have completed this, answer this question: Did Prince Gautama discover 'the truth' because he was a very clever person who was willing to devote himself to discipline and meditation, or was there something in truth which revealed itself when he reached a certain point? Find out what you can about what Buddhists believe.

---

6   Muslims believe that it was necessary for Allah (the Muslim term or name for God) to reveal his truth. He chose a camel driver called Muhammad to learn and recite the truth spoken to him by the Angel Gabriel. When he had learned by heart what the Angel told him, he passed this on to his family and followers and the words were written down in the Holy Qur'an.

Muslims therefore believe that the Qur'an is the pure word of God and that it is the only pure book of its kind. The Qur'an was given in Arabic. In this English translation the Qur'an tells the first words learned by the Prophet:

The Qur'an
96.1f

Recite in the name of your Lord who creates
Creates man from a clot of blood
Recite and your Lord is the most Bountiful One
Who taught by the pen
Taught man what he knew not

Later, the following words were given:

The Qur'an
55.1f

The Beneficent
Taught the Qur'an
He created man
Taught him articulate speech
The sun and moon pursue their ordered course
And the herbs and the trees adore (Him)

Try to find out by talking to a Muslim why no picture must ever be drawn which shows the revelation to Muhammad. Look at some of the books on world religions in your school to see if there are any which break this rule. If they are wrong in this respect, are there other things which are wrong about the books? Find out more about the Muslim faith by using a book written by a Muslim such as G. Sarwar, *Islam – Beliefs and Practices*. Try to get a copy of the Qur'an in translation (preferably by a Muslim translator) and write a paragraph which expresses your reaction to it.

7

Christians believe that it was necessary for God to come to this world in person. It was not simply so that there could be no mistake about the truth but that we could be shown how to live the life God taught about, and so that the problem of human sin which underlies ignorance could be removed too.

The following extract is from one of the four Gospels in the New Testament section of the Holy Bible. It explains that Jesus was God:

The Bible
John chapter 1

There are several ways of translating this passage, as can be seen by comparing different versions of the Bible.

In the beginning was the Word, and the Word was with God, and the Word was God. He was with God in the Beginning.

Through him all things were made; without him nothing was made that has been made. In him was life, and that life was the light of men. The light shines in the darkness, but the darkness could not put it out . . .

The true light that gives light to every man was coming into the world.

He was in the world, and though the world was made by him, the world did not recognise him. He came to that which was his own, but his own people did not receive him. Yet all who received him, to those who believed in his name, he gave the right to become children of God . . .

The Word became flesh and lived for a while among us.

At the beginning of the fourth century CE, Christians wrote
down their beliefs as a test to ensure that Christians held
orthodox beliefs. In the Nicene Creed, there is a clear
statement of belief about Jesus:

We believe in . . .
One Lord Jesus Christ, the only begotten Son of God,
Begotten of the Father before all ages,
Light of Light, true God of true God, begotten not made,
Of one substance with the Father,
Through him all things were made,
Who for us men and our salvation came down from the
heavens and was made flesh of the Holy Spirit and the Virgin
Mary, and became man, and was crucified for us under
Pontius Pilate, and suffered and was buried, and rose again
on the third day according to the Scriptures, and ascended
into the heavens, and sitteth on the right hand of the Father,
and cometh again with glory to judge the living and the dead,
of whose Kingdom there shall be no end.

Try to write a paraphrase or a summary of what each
statement of belief is trying to say. What is it about Jesus
which makes him unique among the leaders or founders of
other world religions? Then find accounts of the life of
Jesus written in the four Gospels of the New Testament
which Christians might use to show that Jesus was really
God in human form.

✡ 2
✡ THE SACREDNESS OF LIFE

Most people know that one of the Ten Commandments in the Jewish Scriptures – the Old Testament of the Bible – says, 'Thou shalt not kill.' It was clear that God did not mean, 'Thou shalt not kill *anything*', because certain things could be killed. It was therefore accepted that the commandment means, 'Thou shalt commit no murder', and it has been written like this in many translations of the Bible.

Look up the following references in the Jewish Law in the Old Testament and begin a list of those things/people which could be killed; continue the list with any other examples you can find:

> Exodus chapter 21, verse 12
> Exodus 21:16–17
> Exodus 21:29
> Leviticus 20:2
> Leviticus 20:12

We live at a time when human life has become 'cheap'. In the extracts which follow, human beings are deliberately killed – in a wartime situation, in order to preserve a man's dignity, and for medical research.

In the first extract, from *The Cruel Sea*, Monsarrat vividly brings out the horrors of war. A tanker has just been torpedoed and has gone up in flames. Survivors are swimming towards HMS *Compass Rose* when Ericson, the captain, is informed that the submarine responsible for the sinking of the tanker has been picked up on the detection apparatus. Does he save the men in the sea now, or save the lives of others who would die if the submarine were allowed to escape? This is the difficult decision he has to make:

Nicholas
Monsarrat
The Cruel Sea

The Captain drew in his breath sharply at the sight. There were about forty men in the water, concentrated in a small space: if he went ahead with the attack he must, for certain, kill them all. He knew well enough, as did everyone on board, the effect of depth-charges exploding under water – the splitting crash which made the sea jump and boil and spout skywards, the aftermath of torn seaweed and dead fish which always littered the surface after the explosion. Now there were men instead of fish and seaweed, men swimming towards him in confidence and hope . . . And yet the U-boat was there, one of the pack which had been harassing and bleeding them for days on end, the destroying menace which *must* have priority, because of what it might do to other ships and other convoys in the future: he could hear the echo on the relay-loudspeaker, he acknowledged Lockhart's developed judgment where the asdic-set was concerned. As the seconds sped by, and the range closed, he fought against his doubts, and against the softening instinct of mercy: the book said: 'Attack at all costs', and this was a page out of the book, and the men swimming in the water did not matter at all, when it was a question of bringing one of the killers to account.

But for a few moments longer he tried to gain support and confidence for what he had to do.

'What's it look like now, Number One?'

'The same, sir – solid echo – exactly the right size – *must* be a U-boat.'

'Is it moving?'

'Very slowly.'

'There are some men in the water, just about there.'

There was no answer. The range decreased as *Compass Rose* ran in: they were now within six hundred yards of the swimmers and the U-boat, the fatal coincidence which had to be ignored.

'What's it look like now?' Ericson repeated.

'Just the same – seems to be stationary – it's the strongest contact we've ever had.'

'There are some chaps in the water.'

'Well, there's a U-boat just underneath them.'

All right, then, thought Ericson, with a new unlooked-for access of brutality to help him: all right, we'll go for the U-boat. With no more hesitation he gave the order: 'Attacking – stand by!' to the depth-charge positions aft: and having made his sickening choice he swept in to the attack with a deadened mind, intent only on one kind of kill, pretending there was no other.

Many of the men in the water waved wildly as they saw what was happening: some of them screamed, some threw themselves out of the ship's path and thrashed furiously in the hope of reaching safety: others, slower-witted or nearer to exhaustion, still thought that *Compass Rose* was speeding to their rescue, and continued to wave and smile almost to their last moment . . . The ship came in like an avenging angel, cleaving the very centre of the knots of swimmers: the amazement and horror on their faces was reflected aboard *Compass Rose*, where many of the crew, particularly among the depth-charge parties aft, could not believe what they were being called upon to do. Only two men did not share this horror: Ericson, who had shut and battened down his mind except to a single thought – the U-boat they must kill: and Ferraby, whose privilege it was to drop the depth-charges. 'Serve you bloody well right!' thought Ferraby as *Compass Rose* swept in among the swimmers, catching some of them in her screw, while the firing-bell sounded and the charges rolled over the stern or were rocketed outwards from the throwers: 'Serve you right – you nearly killed us last night, making us stop next door to that fire – now it's our turn.'

There was a deadly pause, while for a few moments the men aboard *Compass Rose* and the men left behind in her wake stared at each other, in pity and fear and a kind of basic disbelief; and then with a huge hammer-crack the depth charges exploded.

Mercifully the details were hidden in the flurry and roar of the explosion; and the men must all have died instantly, shocked out of life by the tremendous pressure of the sea thrown up upon their bodies. But one freak item of horror impressed itself on the memory. As the tormented water leapt upwards in a solid grey cloud, the single figure of a man was tossed high on the very plume of the fountain, a puppet figure of whirling arms and legs seeming to make, in death, wild gestures of anger and reproach. It appeared to hang a long time in the air, cursing them all, before falling back into the boiling sea.

When they ran back to the explosion area, with the asdic silent and the contact not regained, it was as if to some aquarium where poisoned water had killed every living thing.

Men floated high on the surface like dead goldfish in a film of blood.

In the second extract from *One Flew Over the Cuckoo's Nest*, Chief Bromden, one-half American Indian, tells the story of a ward in a mental institution in the United States which is ruled by 'Big Nurse' who literally holds the lives of the patients in her hands. If they will not conform to her wishes, she arranges very unpleasant treatment.

Her rule is challenged by McMurphy, who arrives from a Labour Camp. Not only does he stimulate his colleagues in the ward so that they begin to act like human beings again, but he directly challenges the nurse by breaking her rules and by taking violent action.

But he does not win. After failing to subdue him by Electric Shock Therapy in which an electric current is passed through the brain, damaging the brain cells, she arranges for him to receive brain surgery which has the effect of taking away his character and initiative, so that he becomes little more than a vegetable. When Chief Bromden realizes what has happened to his friend, he decides that it is wrong to allow him to live in such a sub-human state:

Ken Kesey
One Flew Over the Cuckoo's Nest

. . . I watched and tried to figure out what (McMurphy) would have done. I was only sure of one thing: he wouldn't have left something like that sit there in the day room with his name tacked on it for twenty or thirty years so the Big Nurse could use it as an example of what can happen if you buck the system. I was sure of that.

I waited that night until the sounds in the dorm told me everybody was asleep, and until the black boys had stopped making their rounds. Then I turned my head on the pillow so I could see the bed next to mine. I'd been listening to the breathing for hours, since they had wheeled the Gurney in and lifted the stretcher onto the bed, listening to the lungs stumbling and stopping, then starting again, hoping as I listened they would stop for good – but I hadn't turned to look yet.

There was a cold moon at the window, pouring light into the dorm like skim milk. I sat up in bed, and my shadow fell across the body, seeming to cleave it in half between the hips and the shoulders, leaving only a black space. The swelling had gone down enough in his eyes that they were open; they stared into the full light of the moon, open and undreaming, glazed from being open so long without blinking until they were like smudged fuses in a fuse box. I moved to pick up the pillow, and the eyes fastened on the movement and followed me as I stood up and crossed the few feet between the beds.

The big, hard body had a tough grip on life. It fought a long time against having it taken away, flailing and thrashing around so much I finally had to lie full length on top of it and scissor the kicking legs with mine while I mashed the pillow into the face. I lay there on top of the body for what seemed days. Until the thrashing stopped. Until it was still a while and had shuddered once and was still again. Then I rolled off. I lifted the pillow, and in the moonlight I saw the expression hadn't changed from the blank, dead-end look the least bit, even under suffocation. I took my thumbs and pushed the lids down and held them till they stayed. Then I lay back on my bed.

In the final extract we meet Martin Philips, a doctor at the Hobson University Medical Center in New York, responsible for teaching students and for treatment involving the study of the inner parts of the brain. In the course of his work, he discovered that a number of young women who at one time attended a hospital clinic have completely disappeared. As the story builds up, he finds that the women (or what is left of them) are being used in a top-secret experiment to link the human brain with a set of computers:

Robin Cook
Brain

Martin staggered under the impact of what he saw. The old labs with their small rooms and slate-top experiment tables had been removed. Instead, Philips found himself in a hundred-foot-long room with no windows. Down the centre was a row of huge glass cylinders filled with a clear liquid.

'This is our most valuable and productive preparation,' said Michaels, patting the side of the first cylinder. 'Now I know your first impression will be emotional. It was for all of us. But believe me, the rewards are worth the sacrifice.'

Martin slowly began to walk round the container. It was at least six feet high and three feet in diameter. Inside, submerged in what Martin later learned was cerebrospinal fluid, were the living remains of Katherine Collins. She floated in a sitting position with her arms suspended over her head. A respiration unit was functioning, indicating that she was alive. But her brain had been completely exposed. There was no skull. Most of the face was gone except for the eyes, which had been dissected free and covered with contact lenses. An endotracheal tube issued from her neck.

Her arms had also been dissected to extract the ends of the sensory nerves. These nerve endings looped back like strands of a spider web to connect with electrodes buried within the brain.

Philips made a slow complete circle of the cylinder. An awful weakness spread over him and his legs threatened to give way . . .

'Now listen,' said Michaels. 'I know it's shocking when you first see it. But this scientific breakthrough is so big that it is inconceivable to contemplate the immediate benefits. In medicine alone, it will revolutionise every field. You're going to have to make a decision.'

'What kind of decision?' Martin said, tiredly.

'You're going to have to decide if you can live with this whole affair. I know it is a shock. I confess that I was not going to tell you how we were making our breakthroughs. But since you learned enough to be nearly liquidated, you had to know. Listen, Martin. I am aware that the technique of experimenting on humans without their consent, especially when they must be sacrificed, is against any traditional concept of medical ethics. But I believe the results justify the methods. Seventeen young women have unknowingly sacrificed their lives. That is true. But it has been for the betterment of society and the future guarantee of defence superiority of the United States. From the point of view of each subject, it is a great sacrifice. But from the point of view of two hundred million Americans, it is a very small one. Think of how many women wilfully take their lives each year, or how many people will kill themselves on the highways, and to what end? Here these seventeen women have added something to society, and they have been treated with compassion. They have been well cared for and have experienced no pain. On the contrary, they have experienced pure pleasure.'

1   Draw annotated sketches to show what you understand by the following:

> '. . . the effect of depth-charges exploding under water'
> 'solid echo – exactly the right size', 'the asdic silent and the contact not regained'
> 'they had wheeled the Gurney in and lifted the stretcher on the bed'
> 'submerged in . . . cerebrospinal fluid, were the living remains of Katherine Collins.'

2   Each writer in his own way brings out some of the issues involved when human life is taken:

> ● 'Ericson, who had shut and battened down his mind . . .' This indicates something of the human conflict which is involved.
> ● 'The big, hard body had a tough grip on life. It fought a long time against having it taken away . . .' This indicates that most people do not want to die.
> ● 'An awful weakness spread over him and his legs threatened to give way . . .' This indicates the horror of the situation.

Read through the extracts carefully and identify ways in which each author brings out these and other issues involved in the taking of human life.

3   Look at the descriptive passages in each extract: of the men in the water as Compass Rose moves in to destroy the U-boat; of the description of McMurphy's face with Chief Bromden's shadow falling across his body in the hospital; and of the human remains in the cylinders.
What do the descriptions help you to see and feel?
Can you draw what the author was seeking to convey?

4   In the introduction to the extracts it is suggested that 'human life has become "cheap".' Answer the following questions:

4.1   What evidence is there that human life has become 'cheap'?

4.2   Was human life 'cheap' when people were made to work in industry with no protection from industrial diseases?
Was life 'cheap' when the poor were given inadequate food, clothes and housing to enable them to live?
Was human life 'cheap' when whole cities of non-combatants were slaughtered in ancient warfare?

4.3 What factors cheapen human life?
What might be done to help people value human life more?

4.4 Has human life always been 'cheap'?

4.5 Do the media affect our views of human life? Analyse TV
news and feature programmes over a week and record the
number of instances of death and violence to human life.
Do you think TV violence affects people's attitudes toward
others?
Does it simply reflect what is already there, reinforce
attitudes, or actively encourage people to believe that
violence is normal?

4.6 In *The Cruel Sea*, Ferraby swears as he prepares the depth
charges.
Do you think swearing in a story gives realism, or is it
completely unnecessary?
Is swearing a form of verbal violence?
Why do you think Jesus taught that we should leave things
at 'Yes' and 'No' because anything which goes beyond this
is evil? (Look in the New Testament at Matthew chapter 5,
verse 37.)

---

5 Consider the following situations:
● A mother-to-be knows that she will die if she has her
baby. The only way to save her life is to abort the baby.
(This is one of the rare cases where the mother's death
is a certainty.)
● An army commander knows that the only way to save
a town from the enemy advance is to deploy 10,000
men in a new action, but to do so will result in heavy
loss of life.
● An elderly patient has been on a hospital's life-support
machine for a week without regaining consciousness
following an operation. The doctor learns that an
ambulance is bringing a motorcycle accident case to
the hospital and the only way to save the young life is to
put him on the life-support machine.
● Five soldiers have been told to form a firing squad to
execute a spy during wartime.

Consider these questions in a group before writing down
individual answers:
● If life is taken in each case, is it murder? (Go back to the
list of Bible references you looked at in the beginning of
this work.)
● What principles might we draw up to decide when the
taking of human life is murder and when it is not?

Is it right to try to find which lives might be more 'valuable' than others, or is all human life of equal value?

---

6   Hold a 'Balloon Debate'. Six people are in the basket of a hot air balloon, which is steadily falling towards the sea, and will mean death for them all. The only way to save the balloon and five people is for one person to be thrown over the side. In a balloon debate, six people take on the roles of the six balloonists, and each argues his or her case for remaining in the balloon. After all the claims are heard, a vote is taken to decide who is thrown over the side.

3
CRIME AND PUNISHMENT

Older people often say that they got away with things
which children can never get away with now. This was
because their pranks and crimes were dealt with by the
'extended family'. The extended family was the community
where a person lived.

Laurie Lee lived in a Cotswold village about eighty
years ago and tells of his first sex experiences –
experiences which might get him into real trouble today.
He describes what happened, and then comments on the
changes in authority:

Laurie Lee
Cider with Rosie

Close under the yews, in the heavy green evening, we sat
ourselves solemnly down. The old red trees threw arches
above us, making tunnels of rusty darkness. Jo, like a slip of
yew, was motionless; she neither looked at me nor away. I
leant on one elbow and tossed a stone into the trees, heard it
skipping from branch to branch.

'What shall we do then, Jo?' I asked.

She made no reply, as usual.

'What d'you say, Jo?'

'I don't mind.'

'Come on – you tell.'

'No, you.'

The pronouncement had always to come from me. She
waited to hear me say it. She waited, head still, staring
straight before her, tugging gently at a root of weed.

'Good morning, Mrs Jenkins!' I said breezily. 'What
seems to be the trouble?'

Without a blink or a word Jo lay down on the grass and
gazed up at the red-berried yews, stretched herself subtly on
her green crushed bed, and scratched her calf, and waited.

25

The game was formal and grave in character, its ritual rigidly patterned. Silent as she lay, my hands moved as silently, and even the birds stopped singing.

Her body was pale and milk-green on the grass, like a birch-leaf lying in water, slightly curved like a leaf and veined and glowing, lit faintly from within its flesh. This was not Jo now but the revealed unknown, a labyrinth of naked stalks, stranger than flesh, smoother than candle-skins, like something thrown down from the moon. Time passed, and the cool limbs never moved, neither towards me nor yet away; she just turned a grass ring around her fingers and stared blindly away from my eyes. The sun fell slanting and struck the spear-tipped grass, laying tiger-stripes round her hollows, binding her body with crimson bars, and moving slow colours across her.

Night and home seemed far away. We were caught in the rooted trees. Knees wet with dew I pondered in silence all that Jo's acquiescence taught me. She shivered slightly and stirred her hands. A blackbird screamed into a bush . . .

'Well, that'll be all, Mrs Jenkins,' I said. 'I'll be back again tomorrow.'

I rose from my knees, mounted an invisible horse, and cantered away to supper. While Joe dressed quietly and dawdled home, alone among the separate trees.

Of course, they discovered us in the end; we must have thought we were invisible. 'What about it, young lad? You and Jo – last night? Ho, yes! we seen you, arf! arf!' A couple of cowmen had stopped me in the road; I denied it, but I wasn't surprised. Sooner or later one was always caught out, but the thing was as readily forgotten; very little in the village was either secret or shocking, we merely repeated ourselves. Such early sex-games were formal exercises, a hornless charging of calves; but we were certainly lucky to live in a village, the landscape abounded with natural instruction which we imitated as best we could; if anyone saw us they laughed their heads off – and there were no magistrates to define us obscene.

This advantage was shared by young and old, was something no town can know. We knew ourselves to be as corrupt as any other community of our size – as any London street, for instance. But there was no tale-bearing then or ringing up 999; transgressors were dealt with by local opinion, by silence, lampoons, or nicknames. What we were spared from seeing – because the village protected itself – were the crimes of our flesh written cold in a charge sheet, the shady arrest, the police-court autopsy, the headline of the magistrate's homilies.

As for us boys, it is certain that most of us, at some stage or other of our growth, would have been rounded up under present law, and quite a few shoved into reform school. Instead we emerged – culpable it's true – but unclassified in criminal record. No wilder or milder than Battersea boys, we were less ensnared by by-laws. If caught in the act, we got a quick bashing; the fist of the farmer we'd robbed of apples or eggs seemed more natural and just than any cold-mouthed copper adding one more statistic for the book. It is not crime that has increased, but its definition. The modern city, for youth, is a police-trap.

---

1   Use *all* the evidence in the extract to answer the following questions:

1.1 What game were the children playing?

1.2 How old were the children?

1.3 What time of the year was it?

1.4 What time of the day was it?

1.5 Where were they?

---

2   Laurie Lee describes the surroundings and what was happening by using descriptions of something else. Find the following phrases:

   'making tunnels of rusty darkness'
   'her green crushed bed'
   'like a birch leaf lying in water'
   'smoother than candle-skins, like something thrown
      from the moon'
   'binding her body with crimson bars'

What is he actually describing in each case? Describe what he saw in your own words without using descriptions of something else.

3   Discuss the following together, and then write down your thoughts:

  3.1 What purpose do you think the game had for Laurie Lee? Did it have any purpose for Jo?

  3.2 Think back to your own childhood to some of the imaginative games you used to play. Describe them and say what purpose and value you think they had.

  3.3 Do you think that their purpose has ever been fulfilled?

  3.4 How should our thinking about this guide us when we are buying toys for young children?

4   Re-read the last three paragraphs, and note the following phrases:

> 'there were no magistrates to define us obscene'
> 'the police court autopsy'
> 'the headline of the magistrate's homily'
> 'it is not crime which has increased, but its definition'
> 'The modern city, for youth, is a police-trap'

  4.1 What is Laurie Lee trying to say through each of these phrases about crime and punishment?

  4.2 Do you think that local justice ('the fist of the farmer', 'they laughed their heads off') is better than justice in a magistrate's court?

  4.3 Does your thinking have any relevance to what should be done when school rules are broken? Is corporal punishment better or worse than suspension?

5   Now look at an example of 'justice' as it actually happened in a school. *The Thorn Birds* describes the life of a family on an Australian sheep station through several generations. About a hundred years ago, Meghann (or Meggie) was taken for her first day at the local convent school by her brothers. She was only five years old and became sick with the excitement, so that they were all late for school. This led to discipline from Sister Agatha:

Colleen
McCullough
The Thorn Birds

Crimson marks were etched into the sides of her nose from the remorseless grip of her round, steel-framed spectacles, and behind them her eyes peered out suspiciously, pale-blue and bitter.

'Well, Robert Cleary, why are you late?' Sister Agatha barked in her dry, once Irish voice.

'I'm sorry, Sister,' Bob replied woodenly, his blue-green eyes still riveted on the tip of the quivering cane as it waved back and forth.

'Why are you late?' she repeated.

'I'm sorry, Sister.'

'This is the first morning of the new school year, Robert Cleary, and I would have thought that on this morning if not on others you might have made an effort to be on time.'

Meggie shivered, but plucked up her courage. 'Oh, please, Sister, it was my fault!' she squeaked.

The pale blue eyes deviated from Bob and seemed to go through and through Meggie's very soul as she stood there gazing up in genuine innocence, not aware she was breaking the first rule of conduct in a deadly duel which went on between teachers and pupils *ad infinitum*: never volunteer information. Bob kicked her swiftly on the leg and Meggie looked at him sideways, bewildered.

'Why was it your fault?' the nun demanded in the coldest tones Meggie had ever heard.

'Well, I was sick all over the table and it went right through to my drawers, so Mum had to wash me and change my dress, and I made us all late,' Meggie explained artlessly.

Sister Agatha's features remained expressionless, but her mouth tightened like an overwound spring, and the tip of the cane lowered itself an inch or two. 'Who is this?' she snapped to Bob, as if the object of her enquiry were a new and particularly obnoxious species of insect.

'Please, Sister, she's my sister Meghann.'

'Then in future you will make her understand that there are certain subjects we do not ever mention, Robert, if we are true ladies and gentlemen. On no account do we ever, ever mention by name any item of our underclothing, as children from a decent household would automatically know. Hold out your hands, all of you.'

'But, Sister, it was my fault!' Meggie wailed as she extended her hands palms up, for she had seen her brothers do it in pantomime at home a thousand times.

'Silence!' Sister Agatha hissed, turning on her. 'It is a matter of complete indifference to me which one of you was responsible. You are all late, therefore you must all be punished. Six cuts.' She pronounced the sentence with monotonous relish.

Terrified, Meggie watched Bob's steady hands, saw the long cane whistle down almost faster than her eyes could follow, and crack sharply against the center of his palms, where the flesh was soft and tender. A purple welt flared up immediately; the next cut came at the junction of fingers and palm, more sensitive still, and the final one across the tips of the fingers, where the brain has loaded the skin down with more sensation than anywhere else save the lips. Sister Agatha's aim was perfect. Three more cuts followed on Bob's other hand before she turned her attention to Jack, next in line. Bob's face was pale but he made no outcry or movement, nor did his brothers as their turns came; even quiet and tender Stu.

As they followed the upward rise of the cane above her own hands Meggie's eyes closed involuntarily, so she did not see the descent. But the pain was like a vast explosion, a scorching, searing invasion of her flesh right down to the bone; even as the ache spread tingling up her forearm the next cut came, and by the time it had reached her shoulder the final cut across her fingertips was screaming along the same path, all the way through to her heart. She fastened her teeth in her lower lip and bit down on it, too ashamed and too proud to cry, too angry and indignant at the injustice of it to dare open her eyes and look at Sister Agatha; the lesson was sinking in, even if the crux of it was not what Sister Agatha intended to teach.

It was lunchtime before the last of the pain died out of her hands. Meggie had passed the morning in a haze of fright and bewilderment, not understanding anything that was said or done.

---

6   What words and phrases are used in the story to show that:

- Sister Agatha was a cruel person?
- Sister Agatha did not understand young children?
- Sister Agatha was class conscious?
- The punishment was an act of great cruelty?

When the author says 'the lesson was sinking in', what lesson had Meggie really learned through her punishment?

7

Several reasons are given to explain why people should be punished when they do wrong:

- People should pay for what they do; they deserve it.
- People who commit crimes should be put in a position where they cannot do it again.
- People who do wrong should be punished so that it puts off others from doing the same kind of thing.
- Punishment should help people so that they don't want to do it again.
- Punishment should be given so that the law is upheld.

Now answer these questions:

7.1 Deterrence, reform, retribution, protection, vindication. Which word describes each explanation for punishment?

7.2 Which reasons do you think Sister Agatha would have given for punishing the Cleary family?

7.3 When Laurie Lee said, 'If we were caught in the act we got a quick bashing', what explanation for punishment applied?

7.4 What reasons do you think are the right ones for punishing a person?

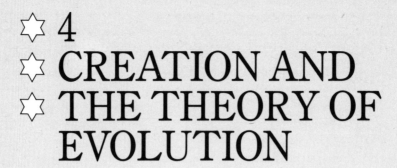

☆ 4
☆ CREATION AND
☆ THE THEORY OF
EVOLUTION

When Charles Darwin was born, it was commonly accepted in the Christian church that God made every kind or species of animal life separately. Every creature was created by God and then reproduced its own kind.

When Darwin worked as naturalist on the survey ship *Beagle*, he began to feel that this was impossible because there were so many varieties of birds and other creatures. God may have started things off, he thought, but then some kind of principle or law came into operation which gave rise to the millions of varieties in nature. He also discovered that some of the forms of life which he had believed God had made were now extinct. How could a caring creator God allow this to happen?

Darwin was very close to his wife, Emma, who was a committed Christian. Irving Stone, in his biography of Charles Darwin, describes what happened when she realized where his thinking was leading him:

Irving Stone
The Origin

What brought the problem to a climax was a long discussion he had late one afternoon with Lyell which he reported in his notebook and, later that evening, to Emma:

'Lyell remarked that species never reappear when once extinct. He suggests that from the remotest periods there has been ever a coming in of new organic forms. My own studies and observations substantiate this. Lyell also suggests that there has been an extinction of those forms which pre-existed on the earth. Such as the Megatherium fossils I found in South America.'

Emma looked up with a disturbed expression.

'Are you suggesting that there is no God?'

'I am suggesting that God, in the beginning, created certain laws. Then He retired, allowing His laws to work themselves out.'

It was the first time he noticed Emma's concern. But he was not prepared for the sequel. The following night, as they were undressing for bed, she said quietly:

'Charles, my dear, I have put a letter on your desk. Well, not really a letter, rather a communication. Would you prefer to read it tonight, or perhaps tomorrow morning?'

'It's the first time since we've been married that you've written me a communication. I had better get to it at once.'

He donned a robe, went into his study, picked up Emma's 'communication', written in her precise manner.

'Too precise,' he thought. 'Emma must have rewritten this several times.'

The state of mind that I wish to preserve with respect to you, is to feel that while you are acting conscientiously and sincerely wishing and trying to learn the truth, you cannot be wrong, but there are some reasons that force themselves upon me, and prevent myself from being always able to give myself this comfort. I daresay you have often thought of them before, but I will write down what has been in my head, knowing that my own dearest will indulge me . . .

May not the habit in scientific pursuits of believing nothing till it is proved, influence your mind too much in other things which cannot be proved in the same way? And which if true are likely to be above our comprehension? I should say also there is a danger in giving up Revelation which does not exist on the other side, that is the fear of ingratitude in casting off what has been done for your benefit as well as for that of all the world, and which ought to make you still more careful, perhaps even fearful lest you should not have taken all the pains you could to judge truly . . .

I do not wish for any answer to all this – it is a satisfaction to me to write it. Don't think that it is not my affair and that it does not much signify to me. Everything that concerns you concerns me and I should be most unhappy if I thought we did not belong to each other forever. I am rather afraid my own dear will think I have forgotten my promise not to bother him, but I am sure he loves me, and I cannot tell him how happy he makes me and how dearly I love him and thank him for all his affection which makes the happiness of my life more and more every day.

He felt the tears roll down his cheeks at Emma's expression of love for him as well as her anxiety over his danger if he lost God and the promise of everlasting life. She had written of her fear of his 'giving up Revelation' and his 'casting off what had been done for his benefit, as well as that of all the world', obviously by God Almighty.

His mind was awhirl. He sat at his desk for an interminable time, then paced his study. When he looked into the bedroom he saw that Emma was fast asleep. She had done her duty as she saw it; it enabled her to achieve tranquility. He kissed the letter for the intensity and wholeness of her love, then stood at the window of his study overlooking the dark garden. What was he to do? He could not go on with his work on the origin and fallibility of species if that work frightened his wife. It would be a sword in the side of their marriage, with perhaps a serious enough wound to destroy it.

---

1   Charles Darwin faced two intellectual puzzles:

- There were millions of varieties of living things. Did God make every one, or did he make some, and then let them develop into all kinds of varieties according to some natural law?
- Some living things have become extinct. We know of their previous existence from fossils. Did God let them die out after he had made them, or is the explanation that they served their purpose in some line of development according to some natural law, and then died out when their purpose had been fulfilled?

His friend Charles Lyell instigated a further puzzle:

- If varieties of living things develop and die out, why should this not be extended to different groups of animals? Why could God not have created an early, simple form of life, and let it develop into the different types of living creatures, as well as their varieties?

At this point in his life, Darwin came to believe that in each generation of creatures, those whose characteristics best suited their environment (because they were stronger in hunting food, or could run faster to escape predators, or were darker in colour to escape detection, or had warmer coats to avoid cold . . . etc) survived to produce the next generation which would to some degree take on the characteristics of the survivors.

The view which Charles Darwin held at this time would be called 'Theistic Evolution' – evolution which is planned by and controlled by God. Emma Darwin believed she could see that this would lead to a belief that there was something in nature itself which would promote such development and therefore there would be no need to believe that God had any part in it. (This belief strictly speaking is called 'Atheistic Evolution'.)

Theistic Evolutionists have argued that there are three factors which show that evolution is not just a 'chance process':

●Even if it can be shown that life has developed according to an evolutionary process, at some point it had to be started off. God must be involved in the starting-point.
●Not only are there fabulously beautiful things in the organic (and inorganic) world, but human beings have the sensitivity to appreciate them and enjoy them in ways which are not simply related to the need for survival. God must have given us this facility.
●An evolutionary process left to itself would be haphazard, but in fact there seems to be a process at work which leads from the simple to the complex as though a designer is in control. That designer would be God.

Think through Charles Darwin's problems, and the viewpoints of those who hold to Theistic and Atheistic evolution. Set up an argument either with another person, or with two groups of people, to test the strength of both sides of the argument as far as you are able. Then write down a summary of the arguments which have been made.

2

Emma Darwin could see spiritual dangers in her husband's position, and sets them out in the central paragraph of her letter. Her argument is as follows:

●The scientist may adopt the view that only those things which can be observed and measured are true.

●There are some things which cannot be observed and measured in such a scientific way.

●Included among these things are those things which God makes known by revelation; that, for example, as her husband noted, God offers everlasting life to those who believe in him.

●Therefore the scientist might cut himself off from God.

2.1 Consider whether there are things which cannot be the subject of scientific experiment, either because they cannot be measured, or because the attempt to measure would destroy the object. (Could Emma's love, for example, be tested in such a way?)

2.2 Consider what might have to be done to be sure that a 'Revelation' really did come from God and not from some kind of impostor, and then assess the strength of Emma's argument.

---

3 The letter which Emma Darwin wrote to her husband was typical of writing in the Victorian age. Rewrite the letter as it might be written in the 1980s, so as to preserve the following aspects of the original letter:

●she is worried for her husband

●she loves her husband deeply

●she respects the scientific work he is doing to try to uncover the truth about the origin of the great variety of living things

●she is highly intelligent and can present a sustained argument

---

4 Darwin had another problem – see the last two sentences of the extract. Explain in writing what you think he should do. Should he carry on with his work, should he abandon it, or is there a way of compromise?

---

5 The position which Charles Darwin held is often given as an example of what has been called 'the conflict of the Bible with science'. The part of the Bible which is usually referred to is contained in the opening section of the Bible:

The Bible
Genesis
chapters
1 and 2

In the beginning God created the heavens and the earth. Now the earth was formless and empty, darkness was over the surface of the deep, and the Spirit of God was hovering over the waters.

And God said, 'Let there be light,' and there was light. God saw that the light was good, and he separated the light from the darkness. God called the light 'day' and the darkness he called 'night'. And there was evening and there was morning – the first day.

And God said, 'Let there be an expanse between the waters to separate water from water.' So God made the expanse and separated the water under the expanse from the water above it. And it was so. God called the expanse 'sky'. And there was evening and there was morning – the second day.

And God said, 'Let the water under the sky be gathered to one place, and let dry ground appear.' And it was so. God called the dry ground 'land', and the gathered waters he called 'seas'. And God saw that it was good.

Then God said, 'Let the land produce vegetation: seed-bearing plants and trees on the land that bear fruit with seed in it, according to their various kinds.' And it was so. The land produced vegetation: plants bearing seed according to their kinds and trees bearing fruit with seed in it according to their kinds. And God saw that it was good. And there was evening, and there was morning – the third day.

And God said, 'Let there be lights in the expanse of the sky to separate the day from the night, and let them serve as signs to mark seasons and days and years, and let them be lights in the expanse of the sky to give light on the earth.' And it was so. God made two great lights – the greater light to govern the day and the lesser light to govern the night. He also made the stars. God set them in the expanse of the sky to give light on the earth, to govern the day and the night, and to separate light from darkness. And God saw that it was good. And there was evening, and there was morning – the fourth day.

And God said, 'Let the water teem with living creatures, and let birds fly above the earth across the expanse of the sky.' So God created the great creatures of the sea and every living and moving thing with which the water teems, according to their kinds, and every winged bird according to its kind. And God saw that it was good. God blessed them and said, 'Be fruitful and increase in number and fill the water in the seas, and let birds increase on the earth.' And there was evening, and there was morning – the fifth day.

And God said, 'Let the land produce living creatures according to their kinds: livestock, creatures that move along the ground, and wild animals, each according to its kind.' And it was so. God made the wild animals according to their kinds, the livestock according to their kinds, and all the creatures that move along the ground according to their kinds. And God saw that it was good.

Then God said, 'Let us make man in our image, in our likeness, and let them rule over the fish of the sea and the birds of the air, over the livestock, over all the earth, and over all the creatures that move along the ground.'

So God created man in his own image, in the image of God he created him; male and female he created them.

God blessed them and said to them, 'Be fruitful and increase in number; fill the earth and subdue it. Rule over the fish of the sea and the birds of the air and over every living creature that moves on the ground.'

Then God said, 'I give you every seed-bearing plant on the face of the whole earth and every tree that has fruit with seed in it. They will be yours for food. And to all the beasts of the earth and all the birds of the air and all the creatures that move on the ground – everything that has the breath of life in it – I give every green plant for food.' And it was so.

God saw all that he had made, and it was very good. And there was evening, and there was morning – the sixth day.

Thus the heavens and the earth were completed in all their vast array.

By the seventh day, God had finished the work he had been doing; so on the seventh day he rested from all his work. And God blessed the seventh day and made it holy, because on it he rested from all the work of creating that he had done.

Now answer the following questions:

5.1 The third paragraph describes how God made the clouds and the sea. Write out what you think the words are actually saying. Is this a 'scientific' account or is it a 'popular' account, to let people know that God made the clouds and the sea?

5.2 In which country in the world does a new day begin in the evening (at 6.00 p.m. our time), so that the day consists of 'an evening and a morning' rather than a 'night and a day'? What might this tell us about the origin of the writing?

5.3 Look at what happened on each day according to the account, and then complete the following table:

Day	God formed . . .	Day	God filled . . .
1	space	4	
2		5	sky and sea
3	dry land	6	

Would you say that there is one account which goes on from day 1 to day 6, or two parallel accounts between day 1 and day 3, day 4 and day 6?

5.4 God keeps saying things. Some of them are commands which make things happen, but elsewhere he is giving things names. Who do you think God is talking to?

5.5 What is strange about the idea of God having a rest on the seventh day? Could God get tired?

5.6 What other creation stories do you know of from other religions and from other cultures? In what way are these similar to, or different from, this account in Genesis?

5.7 Some people believe that the opening passage in the Bible has been developed from a crude creation myth, possibly from Babylon. In their view the earliest account the Jewish people had, which was developed from their traditions, is in Genesis chapter 2, verses 4–25. At a much later time other Jewish priestly leaders purified the account in line with what they had learned from Babylon. Find out more about this from your teacher or from the library. What do you think about it?

5.8 However the piece of writing originated, what would you consider to be the most important thing that it is saying? Why would this passage be placed at the beginning of the Bible?

5.9 What reactions do you have to the biblical account which tells of God making the world?

---

6   Some people believe that the Hebrew verb which is translated 'to make' in the Genesis 1 passage, should be translated 'to show' – which is normally possible in about one case in twenty. On this basis they have put forward the idea that Genesis 1 is not an account of creation at all, but an account of a revelation about creation which took God six days to give to a man. It was once put this way:

In the days when mankind was very new to the world and very primitive in his thinking, people began to ask, 'Who takes the sun across the sky each day? Who makes the grass grow? Who sends the lightning from the clouds?' They did not ask '*What* does these things . . .' because primitive people always ask 'Who?' and never 'What?' If someone hits you with a snowball unexpectedly and you are angry you become primitive for a moment. So you say, 'Who threw that snowball?' Never 'What caused that snowball to hit me?' God, of course, was the answer to their questions, and because he cared that they knew the truth decided he would tell them that *he* takes the sun across the sky, *he* makes the grass grow and *he* sends the lightning from the clouds.

He needed a man. A man who could hear God speak and would not be overfrightened. A man who could write down what God said. In those days such important writing had to be carved out on tablets of stone. The man needed to be a skilled craftsman. So God met him, maybe by a vision he saw or a voice that he heard. God told him that he wanted people to know that *he* was the creator of the world, and the story was long enough to take six days to write down. 'So bring your tools and a tablet of stone and meet me in the forest. Tomorrow. About this time,' said God. The next day at the appointed time, the writing began.

'I want you to carve this out in your stone,' said God; 'word for word. In the beginning *God* created the heavens and the earth . . . *God* called the light "day" and the darkness he called "night". There, that's finished for today.' The man continued a little, writing, as he had been taught, 'And there was evening, and there was morning – the first day.'

The next day, God had something of a problem. 'How can I let him understand about the watercycle? He doesn't know anything about the clouds and the rain and the sea and how they are connected together. I'll help him by getting him to imagine a solid block of water, divided in the middle. The water lifted up will be the water in the sky, and the water left behind will be the sea.' So God began, 'And *God* said let there be a distance between the waters to separate the waters from the waters . . .' The writer understood that *God* was the One who had made the sky and the sea. He wrote it down, and finished his day's work as he had done the previous day: 'There was evening, and there was morning – the second day.' The third day was very similar, except that he wrote down that *God* had formed the dry land and the vegetation in it, and that God told him there were three more days to go.

'Look,' said God, 'you understand now. I was the One who formed space, formed sky and sea, formed the dry land. In the next three days I want to tell you that it was I that filled them. I filled space with the heavenly bodies, the sky and sea with birds and fish, and the dry land with every other creature, including you.' For three more days the man toiled at his task and wrote how God had filled the areas he had made. At the end of the six days God had something more to say.

'You have worked for me for six long days. Now I am stopping. I have nothing else to show you. You must have a complete day's rest. This day will always be a special day when mankind shall not have to work; it is my gift to mankind.'

Discuss, and then write about, your reactions to this approach to the narrative in Genesis 1.

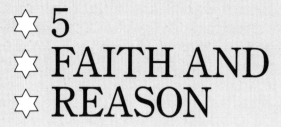

☆ 5
☆ FAITH AND
☆ REASON

People often assume that faith and reason are in conflict, but this need not be true; faith and reason often go together in our daily lives.

When we buy a frozen meal we read the instructions on the box, to find out what we have to do to prepare the food for eating. This is an act of faith but it is not an act of *blind* faith. We believe it is reasonable to follow the instructions on the box because:

- the company producing the food would not be in business if they often gave wrong instructions on their products
- from our past experience the instructions do not look stupid
- when we have followed such instructions before, they have worked

Neither is it true that religious faith need be in conflict with reason. When a religion claims that it can help us to find meaning and purpose in life, we can ask if other people have found it to work — and we can see if the claims of the religion seem consistent with one another.

But there are some cases where there is a conflict between reason and religion. Some religions claim that their truths have been revealed to them directly by God, and therefore the use of reason is inappropriate and inadequate; how could human reason challenge what God has said?

Put another way, there are some things, which ought not to be approached by reason. (If, for example, a person's religious life is looked upon as a relationship with God, the relationship could be destroyed by attempting to put it to the test by reason. This is real enough in human life:

'prove that you love me' might be the very thing which destroys love.) Opponents of religion therefore say that religion has no meaning and so there is a conflict between reason and faith.

Conflict is more common between faith and reason where religious believers have developed what God has said to them into further beliefs of their own. Reason is used to develop their theology.

In the days of the early church it was known by revelation from God that God loved humankind, because this had been stated directly by Jesus. This is not therefore, for the Christian, open to argument. But as Christians thought about this, they argued that if man is so important to God, then the world must be at the centre of the universe, with the sun, moon and planets going round the earth. Their religious reasoning was certainly open to question.

In the two extracts which follow, the conflicts which can arise between faith and reason are brought out. In the first Saleem, a Muslim boy, was born at midnight at the moment that India became a sovereign, independent state. Like other children born at that moment, he received a remarkable supernatural gift – the ability to hold thought conversations with other children born at the same time. It was like 'voices in his head'. Feeling rather proud of his gift, he decided to tell his family, but because it was a strict Muslim family, and what he was saying seemed to say that he was receiving revelations, the reaction was violent:

Salman Rushdie
Midnight's Children

After a period of 'What?' 'Why?' and 'Certainly not', my mother saw something extraordinary sitting in my eyes and went to wake Ahmed Sinai anxiously with, 'Janum, please come. I don't know what has got into Saleem.'

Family and ayah assembled in the sitting-room. Amid cut-glass vases and plump cushions, standing on a Persian rug beneath the swirling shadows of ceiling-fans, I smiled into their anxious eyes and prepared my revelation. This was it; the beginning of the repayment of their investment; my first dividend – first, I was sure, of many . . .

Get it out. Straight, without frills. 'You should be the first to know,' I said, trying to give my speech the cadences of adulthood. And then I told them. 'I heard voices yesterday. Voices are speaking to me inside my head. I think – Ammi, Abboo, I really think – that Archangels have started to talk to me.'

There! I thought. There! It's said! Now there will be pats on the back, sweetmeats, public announcements, maybe more photographs; now their chests will puff up with pride. O blind innocence of childhood! For my honesty – for my open-hearted desperation to please – I was set upon from all sides. Even the Monkey: 'O *God*, Saleem, all this tamasha, all this performance, for one of your stupid *cracks*?' And worse than the Monkey was Mary Pereira[1]: 'Christ Jesus! Save us, Lord! Holy Father in Rome, such blasphemy I've heard today.' And worse than Mary Pereira was my mother Amina Sinai . . . she cried, 'Heaven forfend! The child will bring down the roof upon our heads!' (Was that my fault, too?) And Amina continued: 'You black man! Goonda! O Saleem, has your brain gone raw? What has happened to my darling baby boy – are you growing into a madman – a *torturer*!?' And worse than Amina's shrieking was my father's silence; worse than her fear was the wild anger sitting on his forehead; and worst of all was my father's hand, which stretched out suddenly, thick-fingered, heavy-jointed, strong-as-an-ox, to fetch me a mighty blow on the side of my head, so that I could never hear properly in my left ear after that day; so that I fell sideways across the startled room through the scandalized air and shattered a green tabletop of opaque glass; so that, having been certain of myself for the first time in my life, I was plunged into a green, glass-cloudy world filled with cutting edges, a world in which I could no longer tell the people who mattered most about the goings-on inside my head; green shards lacerated my hands as I entered that swirling universe in which I was doomed, until it was far too late, to be plagued by constant doubts about what I was *for*.

In a white-tiled bathroom beside a washing-chest, my mother daubed me with Mercurochrome; gauze veiled my cuts, while through the door my father's voice commanded, 'Wife, let nobody give him food today. You hear me? Let him enjoy his joke on an empty stomach!'

[1] Mary Pereira worked for the family

In the second extract, Bertholt Brecht, a member of the Communist Party in East Germany, uses drama to look at the conflict which the scientist, Galileo, had with the church, because by using a telescope he had discovered that the earth was not the centre of the universe. He is here talking to a monk who knows the truth about the universe, but who will not accept it or teach it because of its effect upon ordinary believers; he urges Galileo to do the same:

Bertholt Brecht
The Life of Galileo

In the palace of the Florentine Ambassador in Rome.
Galileo is listening to the little monk who whispered the verdict of the Papal astronomers to him after the session of the Collegium Romanum.

Galileo: No no, go on. Talk. The way you're dressed gives you the right to say anything at all.

Little Monk: I have studied mathematics, Signor Galilei.

Galileo: That could come in handy – if it makes you admit now and then that two and two are four.

Little Monk: Signor Galilei, I've not slept for three nights. How can I reconcile the decree of the Holy Office and the moons I see around Jupiter? I decided to say Mass early this morning and come to see you.

Galileo: To tell me the moons of Jupiter aren't there?

Little Monk: No. But I have fathomed the wisdom of the decree. It teaches me there is a danger to mankind in unrestricted scientific research. I have decided to give up astronomy. It is my duty to try to explain the reasons why even an astronomer can abandon his work on the new theories.

Galileo: I know the reasons only too well.

Little Monk: I understand your bitterness. You think of the Church's great powers.

Galileo: Just say instruments of torture.

Little Monk: There are other reasons. Let me speak of myself. I grew up the son of peasants in the Campagna. Simple people. When I observe the phases of Venus I see my family. They sit with my sister by the hearth, eating cheese. I see the roof beams above them, black with the smoke of centuries. I see their work-scarred hands, holding their spoons. Things go badly for them. But in their hardship there is a hidden kind of order. There are the routine cycles of everyday life, from scrubbing the floor, through the seasons in the olive grove, to paying taxes. Whatever the disasters, life is regular. My father's back is not bent suddenly, but a little more with each Spring in the olive grove, just as the births which disfigure my mother's body more and more come at definite intervals. From what do they summon their strength to drag their baskets up the stony path, dripping with sweat, to bear children, even to eat? From the continuity, the sense of necessity, given to them by the sight of the soil, the trees turning green each year, by listening to the Bible texts in the little church each Sunday. They are told God watches them, searchingly, almost anxiously, that the whole theatre of the universe was built around them so that they, the actors, can play their parts well, great or small. What would my family say if I told them that they were really on a small lump of stone, spinning endlessly in empty space around another star, one among many? How can their patience, their submission to misery, be necessary or good? How can the Holy Scriptures be good, explaining and justifying the patience, the hunger and the misery when they're found to be full of lies? No – I see their eyes fill with fear, I see them drop their spoons on the hearth, betrayed and cheated. I hear them say – so, no one watches us, eh? We must look after ourselves, even though we are ignorant, old and worn out, and Nobody has given us a part to play, there is only this miserable earthly life on a tiny star, around which nothing evolves? There is no meaning in our misery, hunger is just not-having-eaten, not a test of strength – hard work is just stooping and tugging, no virtue. So do you understand that I see true, maternal compassion in the Decree of the Holy Congregation, a great goodness of soul?

Galileo: Goodness of soul! What you mean is nothing's left, the wine's been drunk, so let their cracked lips kiss the cassock! Why is nothing left? Why is order in this country the order of an empty larder, and the only necessity that of working yourself to death? Between bursting vineyards, at the edge of full wheatfields? Because your Campagna peasants pay for the wars of the representative of gentle Jesus he wages in Spain and Germany. Why does he put the earth at the centre of the universe? So that Peter's chair can stand at the centre of the earth! That's what it's really about. You're right – it's not about the planets, it's about the peasants of the Campagna. And don't give me that crap about the beauty of traditions, golden with age. Do you know how the Margaritifera oyster produces its pearl? By becoming dangerously ill, enveloping an excruciating body, like a grain of sand, in a ball of slime. It nearly dies. To hell with the pearl – give me the healthy oyster. Virtues don't depend on misery, my friend. If your family were well off and happy, they'd have all the virtues being well off and happy brings. These virtues of exhausted men come from exhausted fields and I reject them. My new water pumps work more miracles than their ridiculous drudgery. 'Be fruitful and multiply' – for the fields are unfruitful and the wars kill your children. Do you want me to lie to your family?

Little Monk, in great irritation: The highest principles compel us to silence – for the peace of mind of suffering humanity!

Galileo: Do you want to see a Cellini clock? Cardinal Bellarmin's coachman delivered it this morning. A perk for not disturbing the peace of mind of suffering humanity. The authorities offer me wine, made sweet with the sweat of your parents' brows – which are, as we all know, created in God's image. If I were prepared to be silent, it would be from really base motives – good living, no persecution, *etcetera*.

Little Monk: Signor Galilei, I am a priest.

Galileo: And a physicist. And you see that Venus has phases. Look out there. (He points out of the window.) See the little Priapus, by the spring next to the laurel? The god of gardens, birds and thieves – boorish, obscene, two thousand years old! He told fewer lies. Forget that, all right, I'm a son of the Church. But do you know Horace's eighth satire? I've been reading him again – for a sense of balance. (He reaches for a small book.) A little statue of Priapus was put up in the Esquiline Gardens. Horace makes it speak.

'A fig-tree log, a useless piece of wood
was I, when the carpenter, uncertain
whether to make a Priapus or a stool
decided on the God.'

Do you think Horace would have let the stool be censored from the poem and a table put in its place? My sense of beauty is wounded if Venus has her phases censored from my view of the universe. We can't invent machines for pumping water up from the river if we're not allowed to look at the greatest machine before our eyes – the heavenly bodies. The sum of the angles of a triangle can't be changed on the whim of the Vatican. I can't calculate the paths of flying bodies to explain the rides of witches on their broomsticks as well.

Little Monk: But won't the truth, if it is the truth, prevail – with us or without us?
Galileo: No. No, no. As much of the truth will prevail that we make prevail. The victory of reason can only be the victory of reasonable people.

---

1   Read the first extract and then answer the following questions:

1.1   What is meant by the terms ayah, Ammi and Abboo?

1.2   What had Saleem said to his mother, Amina, to make her say, 'What?' 'Why?' and 'Certainly not'?

1.3   What evidence is there in the story to show what income-bracket Saleem's family were in?

1.4   Use the words 'revelation', 'cadences', 'shards' and 'lacerate' in four separate sentences, to show that you understand their meaning.

1.5   What religion did Mary Pereira follow? How do we know?

1.6   What did Saleem mean when, looking back later, he said he thought he was helping to repay his parents' investment with their first dividend?

---

2   Write out what you know of Muslim belief about revelation to the prophet Muhammad and how the Holy Qur'an came to be written. Then, in the light of this, explain how the following people in the story viewed Saleem's revelation:

the Monkey (his sister)
Mary Pereira
his mother, Amina Sinai
his father, Ahmed Sinai

When you have done this, discuss as a group the ways in which a person who questioned everything rationally might challenge someone who held the Muslim faith. What reasons might a Muslim give in reply, to show that his faith should not be open to such questions. If it is possible, talk this through with a Muslim. There have been many Christians who have claimed that the rise of rationalism destroyed the power of Christianity. Do you think it possible that Christianity should learn from Islam in this respect?

---

3   **Project:** Find out what you can about the origin of the Bah'ai faith. How are the Bah'ais regarded by strict

Muslims? In what part of the world do Bah'ais suffer persecution? Why is this?

4 Read the extract about Galileo carefully. Explain in a notebook what the phases of Venus are. Explain how these phases, together with the moons of Jupiter, which Galileo saw through his telescope, proved that the earth was not at the centre of the universe.

5 Examine the major speeches by the little monk and by Galileo in the play; then set out the arguments which each put forward to show that it is best that ordinary people do not know that the earth is not at the centre of the universe. Then set out the arguments used by Galileo to show that the church has other reasons for hiding the truth about the universe. Discuss whether or not you think there is any force in the arguments of the little monk, and which of Galileo's arguments enshrine Brecht's own position as a communist writer.

6 Read the final part of the extract from the play, from the point where Galileo tells about the gift of the Cellini clock. Then in your own words write out the following points which are being made:

●Galileo's point that he should no more be asked to leave out the phases of Venus than Horace should be asked to leave out the stool.
●The need to study the universe as a machine in order to develop technology.
●That science is absolutely true and cannot be changed by human opinion, or be relevant to 'religious' beliefs.

Do you think there is any force in the arguments which Brecht has put into Galileo's mouth?

⭐ 6
TO CHURCH ON SUNDAY

For many years it has been a tradition to go to Church on Sundays. In the two extracts which follow we go first with Laura and Edmund to a Methodist service in the Oxfordshire hamlet of Lark Rise about a hundred years ago. In the person of Laura, Flora Thompson describes how she liked to get out of her own cottage on a Sunday evening because nobody was supposed to speak or move whilst her father was reading. She used to go to the Methodist service with her younger brother, Edmund.

In the second extract we go with Peter Jenkins into an American village service. Peter Jenkins was trying to 'find himself' while walking across America; staying with a black family in a trailer in a place called Smokey Hollow, he was taken to their church on a Sunday morning in 1974.

Flora Thompson
Lark Rise to Candleford

The Methodists were a class apart. Provided they did not attempt to convert others, religion in them was tolerated. Every Sunday evening they held a service in one of their cottages, and, whenever she could obtain permission at home, it was Laura's delight to attend . . .

The first thing that would have struck anyone less accustomed to the place was its marvellous cleanliness. The cottage walls were whitewashed and always fresh and clean. The everyday furniture had been carried out to the barn to make way for the long white wooden benches, and before the window with its drawn white blind stood a table covered with a linen cloth, on which were the lamp, a large Bible, and a glass of water for the visiting preacher, whose seat was behind it. Only the clock and a pair of red china dogs on the mantelpiece remained to show that on other days people lived and cooked and ate in the room. A bright fire always glowed in the grate and there was a smell compounded of lavender, lamp-oil, and packed humanity.

The man of the house stood in the doorway to welcome each arrival with a handshake and a whispered 'God bless you!' His wife, a small woman with a slight spinal curvature which thrust her head forward and gave her a resemblance to an amiable-looking frog, smiled her welcome from her seat near the fireplace. In twos and threes, the brethren filed in and took their accustomed places on the hard, backless benches. With them came a few neighbours, not of their community, but glad to have somewhere to go, especially on wet or cold Sundays.

In the dim lamplight dark Sunday suits and sad-coloured Sunday gowns massed together in a dark huddle against the speckless background, and out of it here and there eyes and cheeks caught the light as the brethren smiled their greetings to each other.

If the visiting preacher happened to be late, which he often was with a long distance to cover on foot, the host would give out a hymn from Sankey and Moody's Hymn-Book, which would be sung without musical accompaniment to one of the droning, long-drawn-out tunes peculiar to the community. At other times one of the brethren would break into extempore prayer, in the course of which he would retail the week's news so far as it affected the gathering, prefacing each statement with 'Thou knowest', or 'As thou knowest, Lord'. It amused Laura and Edmund to hear old Mr Barker telling God that it had not rained for a fortnight and that his carrot bed was getting 'mortal dry'; or that swine fever had broken out on a farm four miles away and that his own pig didn't seem 'no great shakes'; or that somebody had mangled his wrist in a turnip cutter and had come out of hospital, but found it still stiff; for, as they said to each other afterwards, God must know already, as He knew everything. But these one-sided conversations with the Deity were conducted in a spirit of simple faith. 'Cast your care upon Him' was a text they loved and took literally. To them God was a loving Father who loved to listen to His children's confidences. No trouble was too small to bring to 'the Mercy Seat'.

Sometimes a brother or a sister would stand up to 'testify', and then the children opened their eyes and ears, for a misspent youth was the conventional prelude to conversion and who knew what exciting transgressions might not be revealed. Most of them did not amount to much. One would say that before he 'found the Lord' he had been 'a regular beastly drunkard'; but it turned out that he had only taken a pint too much once or twice at a village feast; another claimed to have been a desperate poacher, 'a wild, lawless sort o' chap'; he had snared an occasional rabbit. A sister confessed that in her youth she had not only taken a delight in decking out her vile body, forgetting that it was only the worm that perishes; but, worse still, she had imperilled her immortal soul by dancing on the green at feasts and club outings, keeping it up on one occasion until midnight.

Such mild sins were not in themselves exciting, for plenty of people were still doing such things and they could be observed at first hand; but they were described with such a wealth of detail and with such self-condemnation that the listener was for the moment persuaded that he or she was gazing on the chief of sinners. One man, especially, claimed that pre-eminence. 'I wer' the chief of sinners,' he would cry; 'a real bad lot, a Devil's disciple. Cursing and swearing, drinking and drabbing there were nothing bad as I didn't do. Why, would you believe it, in my sinful pride, I sinned against the Holy Ghost. Aye, that I did,' and the awed silence would be broken by the groans and 'God have mercys' of his hearers while he looked round to observe the effect of his confession before relating how he 'came to the Lord'.

No doubt the second part of his discourse was more edifying than the first but the children never listened to it; they were too engrossed in speculations as to the exact nature of his sin against the Holy Ghost, and wondering if he were really as thoroughly saved as he thought himself; for, after all, was not that sin unpardonable? He might yet burn in hell. Terrible yet fascinating thought!

Peter Jenkins
A Walk Across America

. . . After a few awkward minutes, the service started and I realised it was right to compare this church to a shaker. If the church had not been built with strong timbers and bricks, the place would have vibrated apart. The ladies in the choir all dressed in the same brilliant pink, and they numbered about half of the congregation . . .

Reverend Lewis Grant, a young man about my age who drove 150 miles one way every Sunday, stood up. 'It's good to see y'all this day – the Laud's day! Is everybody glad to be in church?' Brother Grant shouted at the top of his lungs.

Everyone but me knew what was coming and answered loud enough to wake up any drunks who were trying to sleep off last night. 'A-man!' As hard as it was for me to believe, they actually meant it. Even the young boys on the back pew were glad to be in church.

'Okay, Roscoe,' Reverend Grant said, 'let's hear y'all sing real good!'

Right on cue, the large choir stood in perfect unison. As dark as the rich black earth that grew the king trees, Roscoe led the choir with gentle nods from his goateed chin, and the crisp, sharp notes from his red electric guitar. The first powerful song the choir sang was 'When I Get to Heaven, I Will Sing and Shout, There'll Be No One There to Turn Me Out'. The gospel cries and shouts blasted forth from their souls so strong that I had goosebumps.

Over to my right, unnoticed by me until now, sat a little lady who looked old enough to be Pau Pau's mother. She was dressed purer than ivory in her white dress and white gloves. Her hair was lily-white and so were her spotless shoes. Her smooth chocolate skin shone from the bright light that filtered through the yellow church windows. There was a cane by her side and she was bent, stooped painfully in half. This was the eighty-year-old Miss Lucy Ann Siler, and mother of the church.

The change that took place in Miss Lucy during the service was a symbol of the whole congregation. When the choir chimed peacefully 'What a Friend We Have in Jesus', the death look that dulled Miss Lucy's face left her. After half the verses were sung, I looked over to make sure she was still alive, only to see she was sitting up much straighter. After the second verse, she was snapping her bony, knotted fingers. When the choir, led by Roscoe, switched to its next song, 'Jesus Will Set You Free', Miss Lucy began to snap her fingers with both hands and move and sway her whole upper body, singing 'A-man, A-man'. Then without warning, Miss Lucy was standing and swaying to the piano and guitar beats without her cane. Her arms stretched upwards as if she were trying to touch heaven, and her face glowed. Next she floated around to my side of the church and started hugging every-one, including red-and-white me. When the hundred-pound black grandmother grabbed me as if I were her grandson, I had a milkshake mixture of feelings about what I was doing in this place. I couldn't believe that feeble little mother of Mount Zion Church, who looked ready to die only moments earlier, was feeling so good after a few songs from the choir. It scared me in a lot of ways, but especially because the preaching had not started yet. I wished I could get out of this place. It was so drastically different from my parents' church back in Connecticut. In the middle of my churning plan to escape, Pau Pau, sitting on my left, looked straight and hard at me and shouted a powerful 'A-man!' I was there to stay after that.

The choir reached to the bottom of their souls and bellowed three or four more songs in unpolished harmony. Afterward, the Rev, as they called Lewis Grant, leaped excitedly to the pulpit. The Rev was a full-time employee at Sears in Ashville, North Carolina, but judging from the way he jumped to the podium to preach, this was his first love. After one sentence I knew it was. I had never heard anyone preach like him. The congregation was not stoic and never silent. After every sentence or Bible verse, the entire church of dark faces would respond, 'A-man'. The two-hour service was like a tide coming. Wave after wave washed through the church and washed the people clean. 'A-man, A-man . . . A-man!'

Instead of making me drowsy, the soul-igniting sermon woke my inner being that had been asleep for twenty-two years. When the radiant preacher stepped down, the church popped with energy and I felt more invigorated than if I had jumped into a cold shower after a steamy sauna. Standing to the side of the platform, the Rev asked all the visitors to stand up. Nervous about being the only white, I hoped there would be some other guests. I wasn't able to hide among the sea of shiny black faces, so I barely sneaked up my noticeable white hand.

The Rev, who had been looking at me the whole time anyway, asked, 'Well, there's a guest . . . Laud bless ya, please stand up!'

Here and now, standing felt worse than having to make a speech to a whole classroom. I was scared of their prejudices and fearful they might make fun of me, but I stood up, mixed breed that I was, shaking and blushing redder by the second.

'Hello, everybody! My name's Peter Jenkins and I'm living down with the Olivers in Smokey Hollow.'

'A-man!' they all sang.

---

1   Draw a picture of the service, write an example of the kind of hymn/music which the congregation might sing, or write part of the sermon you might expect to hear in Lark Rise or Smokey Hollow.

OR:

Describe carefully how the worship at Lark Rise or Smokey Hollow differs from any other form of worship which you have seen or know about.

---

2   Form a group of between six and eight persons and then follow through one of the following investigations. Make a display to show what you have discovered to other groups, and prepare a leaflet to explain the display. The questions are to help you to get started.

2.1 Methodism
● Who were John and Charles Wesley? What was their background and the background of the times they lived in? How were they involved in the start of Methodism?
● Who were the Primitive, United and Wesleyan Methodists?
● What does a modern Methodist church look like and what are the Sunday services like?

2.2 Moody and Sankey
● Who were Dwight Moody and Ira Sankey?
● What is the musical background to the Sankey hymns?
● Where would you find the Sankey hymnbook in use today? Is there any particular kind of church or age-group which is involved?
● What would you expect of the kind of Sunday service where such a hymnbook is in use?

2.3 Black Pentecostal-type churches
● How and where did the modern Pentecostal movement start in church life? Where did it get its name?
● In what way are 'charismatic churches' or 'housegroups' similar to black Pentecostal groups?
● What would you expect if you went to a Pentecostal-type service? What is an Elim Church? What are Assemblies of God? What is the New Testament Church of God?

3   Some people went to the Methodist meeting at Lark Rise because they were 'glad to have somewhere to go, especially on wet or cold Sundays'. Peter Jenkins said that he wished 'I could get out of this place'.

3.1 What is it about church which makes some people feel that they want to go? In what way does a church meet (a) social and (b) spiritual needs?

3.2 What is it about church which puts some people off? Why do some people feel that church is (a) strange and (b) irrelevant?

3.3 Can you think of reasons why there has been a decline in church attendance?

3.4 Do the same principles you have noted in 3.1, 3.2 and 3.3 apply to the gurdwarah, mandir, mosque and synagogue?

---

4   Worship does not have to be religious, although the word is normally used in a religious way. Worship is 'the celebration of those things which have supreme *worth* for us.' 'Worth-ship' might be a better term than 'worship'. We therefore speak of 'his worship the Mayor' because the Mayor is the most important citizen and therefore has greatest worth. We sometimes say 'he worships the very ground she walks upon' because she is the most important person in his life, or even 'baby Philip worships his teddy', because his teddy seems to be the most important toy. 'Sun worshippers' are people who spend as much of their holiday time as possible sunbathing on the beach, lapping up the sun.

4.1 Write three sentences using the word 'worship' in different ways to include at least one religious and one non-religious meaning. Indicate who or what is of greatest worth.

4.2 What picture of God as the Being of greatest worth do you think people had at Lark Rise? (Note: 'its marvellous cleanliness', 'dark Sunday suits', 'Cast your care upon him.')

4.3 What picture of God as the Being of greatest worth do you think people had at Smokey Hollow? (Note: 'in the same brilliant pink', 'the gospel cries and shouts blasted forth from their souls', 'Miss Lucy was standing and swaying to the piano.')

4.4 What features have the services at Lark Rise and Smokey Hollow in common? How do they differ?

4.5 Write down the kind of God you believe in and then write down five different ways of expressing what you believe in a form of worship. If you do not believe in any kind of God, write down five ways of emphasizing the importance of a person who reaches the age of maturity.

5   In the UK the school day is supposed to start with 'an act of collective worship'. Discuss what happens in your school so as to bring out what is really being worshipped, whether what is being done is appropriate and whether it works. You might like to extend this discussion to any other experiences of group worship you know, such as a church service, a service on Remembrance Sunday or a wedding.

If, as in the US public schools, there is no worship in your school, discuss whether it would or would not be a good thing.

6   Comment on the following phrases:
'a table covered with a linen cloth, on which were the lamp, a large Bible, and a glass of water for the visiting preacher'
'dark Sunday suits and sad-coloured Sunday gowns'
'one-sided conversations with the Deity'
'found the Lord'
'a shaker'
'mother of the church'
'Jesus will set you free'
'that feeble little mother of Mount Zion Church'
'the church popped with energy'

☆ 7
GUILT

One way people describe religion is that it is a belief and practice which brings peace between their God and themselves, their neighbours and themselves and their conscience and themselves. So important is religion to a person's inner life that Freud, the psychologist, suggested that religion came into existence because humankind needed to invent a God for their own mental health. When people become conscious of wrong they have done, they have to find some means of coming to terms with the guilt or else it becomes too much for them to bear. The following two extracts show how two very different people dealt with problems of guilt.

The first comes from a novel written by Morris West. He tells how villagers in a remote village in southern Italy believed that a saint lived among them at the end of the 1939–45 war. The Roman Catholic Church could not consider that the local saint be recognized until the whole story had been thoroughly investigated.

In *The Devil's Advocate* West tells how an English priest was sent to the village to find out the story and, as 'devil's advocate', find every possible reason for rejecting it. He found that the man concerned had arrived at the end of the war, and during a long and terrible winter, had comforted and cared for the villagers . . .

Morris West
The Devil's Advocate

They lived like hibernating animals, each litter an island in a sea of snow, drawing warmth from each other's bodies, familiar with each other's stench, munching blindly on the common crust, wondering bleakly how long they would last and whether there would ever be another spring.

If a knock came on the door, they ignored it. Who but thieves or crazy men or starving ones would be abroad at this time? If the knock was persistent, they cursed in chorus, until finally it stopped and they heard the crackling footsteps retreat across the frozen snow. There was only one knock they knew and one voice to which they answered – Giacomo Nerone's.

Every day and all day he was about, making the rounds of the houses – a black-jowled, smiling giant, with his boots wrapped in sacking and his body padded in layers of scarecrow garments and his head muffled in a cap made of one of Nina's stockings. On his back he carried an old army knapsack, filled with rations, and his pockets were stuffed with aspirin tablets and a bottle of cod-liver oil and odds and ends of medicine.

When he came into a house, he stayed as long as they needed him and no longer. He checked their food stocks, looked at the sick, dosed them when he could, cooked a broth for those who were incapable, cleaned up the accumulated messes and then moved on . . .

Always his last call of the day was on Aldo Meyer . . . One evening when it was late and bitter with a new wind, he came in, dumped his sack on Meyer's floor, tossed off the *grappa* at one gulp and said abruptly:

'Meyer, I want to talk to you!'

'You always do,' said Meyer mildly. 'What's so different about tonight?'

Nerone ignored the irony and plunged on.

'I never told you why I came here, did I? . . . Tell me, do you believe in God, Meyer?'

'I was brought up to believe in Him,' said Meyer guardedly. 'My friends the Fascisti have done their best to persuade me otherwise. Let's say I have an open mind on the matter. Why do you ask?'

'I could be talking nonsense to you.'

'It's a man's right to talk nonsense when he has a need.'

'All right. You make what you like of it. I'm English, you know that. I'm an officer, which you didn't know.'

'I guessed it.'

'I'm also a deserter.'

'What do you want me to say?' asked Meyer with dry humour. 'How much I despise you?'

'Say nothing, for God's sake. Just listen. I was in the advance guard for the assault on Messina. It was the last toehold in Sicily. For us, nothing to it. Your people were beaten.

The Germans were pulling out fast. Just a mopping-up operation. My company was assigned to clean out a half-mile square of tenements leading down to the docks. Scattered snipers, a couple of machine-gun posts . . . nothing. There was a blind alley, with windows facing down towards us and a sniper in the top window. He had us pinned down for ten minutes at the mouth of the alley. Then, we thought we might have got him. We moved in. When we got to the house, I followed the usual routine, and shouted a surrender warning. There was another shot – from the lower window this time. It got one of my boys. I pitched a grenade through the window, waited for the burst and then went in. I found the sniper – an old fisherman, with a woman and a nursing child. All dead. The baby had taken the full burst . . .'

'It happens in war,' said Meyer coolly. 'It's the human element. It has nothing to do with God.'

'I know,' said Giacomo Nerone. 'But I was the human element. Can you understand that?'

Anna is a totally different kind of person. A member of a Jewish family in the United States, she and Joseph were happily married with a small child, Maury, but at the time they were very poor. Overwhelmed by fantasies about her former, rich employer, she allowed him to seduce her, and found she was carrying his child. Overcome by remorse and unable to go to the synagogue, she went for solace to the local Roman Catholic church . . .

Belva Plain
Evergreen

'Dear God, listen to me, if the temple were open I would go in there. No, I wouldn't, I'd be afraid someone would see me. Dear God, I don't even know whether I believe in You. I wish I were like Joseph because he believes, he really does. But listen to me anyway, and tell me what I'm to do. I'm twenty-four years old. I have so many years to live through and how am I to get through them?'

Someone asked, 'Are you in trouble, daughter?'

She looked up at the young priest, in his long black robe with the metal chain around his waist. She had never been this close to a priest. At home when you saw one coming down the road you went the other way.

'I'm not a Catholic,' she said. 'I only came in out of the rain.'

'I don't mind. If you want to sit here you're welcome. But perhaps you want to talk?'

A human being, a good face. And she would never see him again.

'I am in such trouble that I want to die,' Anna said.

'Everyone feels that way at some time in his life.' The priest sat down.

How to begin? 'My husband trusts me,' she whispered. *That's a stupid way to start.* 'He tells me I'm the only person in the world he can absolutely trust.'

The priest waited.

'He says he knows I would never lie to him. Never—'

'And you have lied to him?'

'More than that. Oh, more than that!' She could not look at him. Not at the statue or the pictures, either. Down at the floor, at her own hands in her lap. 'How can I tell you? You will think that I am – you will not want to hear, you've never heard—'

'I've heard everything.'

'Not this. I can't say it, no, I can't. But I can't keep it all alone inside, either. Not any longer.'

'Has it to do with the child you're expecting? Is that what you're trying to say?'

She didn't answer.

'It's not his child? Is that it?'

'No,' she whispered. 'Oh my God, I would be better off dead!'

'That's not for you to say. Only God knows whether you would be better off and He will decide, you may be sure.'

'But do I deserve to live?'

'Everything that lives deserves to live. And certainly this child deserves it.'

'I would feel better if I could pay, if I were punished.'

'And you think you won't be? Every day of your life.'

The organ, which had stopped for a time, began again. The quiet music curled like smoke, like mist.

'I've looked for the courage to tell the truth to Joseph. I've prayed for the courage, but it doesn't come.'

'Why must you tell him?'

'To be honest, to feel clean again.'

'At the price of his peace?'

'Do you think it would be?'

'You think about it for a minute.'

But no thoughts came, nothing coherent except the face of her little boy. He was sitting on the kitchen floor eating an apple.

'Is it, perhaps, that you love this other man?'

'No. No, it's my husband I love.' An easy answer. True, and yet . . . Peace and life and goodness; Maury[1], child of my heart; all these, weighed against that short exaltation, that rapture.

She cried out, 'And so I have to go on like this!'

'If you were blind or crippled you would. People do.' The priest sighed. 'Human beings have so much courage, I marvel at how much.'

'I've used up all my courage.'

'You'll find it again. And thank God for giving it back to you.' His voice was even, without reproach or sympathy.

'I hope so.'

'And after a while things will be easier for you.'

'I hope so.'

Perhaps he does know something. He hears and sees so many things. Surely this must have happened before to somebody else?

The priest stood up. 'Do you feel any better?'

'A little,' she answered truthfully. Some of the weight had been relieved, as though she had taken it from herself and put it on him.

'Can you go home now?'

'I think I can. I'll try. I want to thank you,' she whispered.

He raised his hand. His heavy skirt swept down the aisle.

[1]Maury is her child by Joseph

---

1   The extract from Morris West's writing has a number of associated adjectives and nouns like 'hibernating animals', and 'accumulated messes'. Identify the following adjectives and nouns from the passage and describe what they mean:

c_____   f _____

s_____   g_____

d_____   h_____

s_____   s_____

b_____   a_____

Belva Plain's extract has little description because it records a conversation. One thing which is described is the organ: 'The organ which had stopped for a time began again. The quiet music curled like smoke, like mist.' What kind of music do you think was being played? Does it suggest anything about the size or atmosphere of the church?

2 In the two extracts there are a number of technical terms. Use reference books to find out what they mean. Some questions are given below to guide you in the scope of your explanation.

> *grappa:* What is it? Where is it made?
> *Fascisti:* Who were they? What did they believe?
> *Messina:* Where is it? What happened there in the 1939–1945 war?
> *statue:* What kind of statues would you see in a Roman Catholic church building? Why are they there?
> *long black robe:* What is the name given to the long robe worn by a Roman Catholic priest? In what ways are they different from clothes worn by clergy in other churches?

3 Read again the conversation which Giacomo Nerone had with Aldo Meyer. Then answer the following questions:

3.1 Describe Aldo Meyer's first reaction when Nerone entered the house.

3.2 What was Nerone's first action when he was faced by his conscience?

3.3 In what ways might 'running away' or 'distancing oneself from a problem' help a troubled conscience?

3.4 In what way was Nerone's care of the villagers linked to the events in Messina?

3.5 What did Nerone hope to get from Meyer as a result of telling the story?

4 Read again the conversation between Anna and the priest from when she whispers, 'My husband trusts me.' Then answer the following questions:

4.1 Why is it that she cannot actually tell the priest what she has done?
Why could she not look at him?

4.2 There were three easy ways out of the guilt she had, which she believed were open to her:

- to die ('I would be better dead')
- to do something ('I would be better if I could pay')
- to confess to her husband ('. . . to tell the truth to Joseph')

Explain carefully how the priest meets these points and discuss whether you think he was right.

4.3 Why did she feel better after the conversation? What had she gained from the encounter?

---

5 Write a story involving a conflict between good and evil. Use at least eight of the following words in your story:

shame	forgiveness
guilt	pardon
fear	remission
condemnation	absolution
judgment	reconciliation
confession	excuse
sinfulness	exonerate
offence	acquit
unclean	justification
atone	let off

Other words with similar meanings can be found in a thesaurus, which has the opposite function to a dictionary. In a thesaurus we think of an idea, and look it up in the index. The thesaurus then gives us a list of the words which express the idea.

---

6 Different religions offer different ways of approaching human failure and sin. Find out the way it is dealt with in the following religions, using the questions and clues which are given to you. There are reference books on world religions such as *A Lion Handbook: The World's Religions* in most libraries.

Hindu Hindus believe that when we die we will be reborn. How does the present life have an effect on the future one?

Jewish What would you understand by the Jewish religious practice of making a guilt-offering to God?

Christian Find the words of the Christian hymn which was written to explain Easter to children –

'There is a green hill far away
Without a city wall
Where the dear Lord was crucified
Who died to save us all.'

Muslim When, in orthodox Islam, a person is severely
punished for their wrong doing, what is it expected
that this will do?

Discuss in a group the effect each religion might have
upon the life and thinking of a person like Giacomo Nerone
and upon Anna.

MYSTERIES OF SPACE AND TIME

In *The Shepherd* Frederick Forsyth told a Christmas ghost story. It was Christmas Eve, 1957, and a young Royal Air Force pilot left Germany, alone in a Vampire jet, to be home for Christmas. On his way over the North Sea, a main fuse blew on the aircraft and he was left with no compass and no radio. As he approached England, thick fog obliterated the sea and the land ahead, so that he became totally lost and knew that he faced certain death.

It was then that he saw below him another aircraft, a Mosquito bearing the marking, 'JK'. The aircraft acted as a guide, a 'shepherd' down through the fog to a near-deserted airfield in Norfolk, and then disappeared.

Only one officer was on duty over Christmas, but with the help of an old civilian who used to work at the base during the war, he arranged for a meal and accommodation for the young pilot. Nobody knew anything about the pilot or aircraft which had shepherded him to safety but, while he was awaiting his meal, the young pilot recognized the aircraft and the pilot in an old photograph . . .

Frederick
Forsyth
The Shepherd

I halted before an old photograph in a frame standing alone on the mantel above the crackling fire. I stopped with my cigarette half-raised to my lips, feeling the room go suddenly cold.

The photo was old and stained but behind its glass it was still clear enough. It showed a young man of about my own years, in his early twenties, dressed in flying gear. But not the grey suits and gleaming plastic crash helmet of today. He wore thick sheepskin-lined boots, rough serge trousers and a heavy sheepskin zip-up jacket. From his left hand dangled one of the soft-leather flying helmets they used to wear, with goggles attached, instead of the modern pilot's tinted visor.

He stood with legs apart, right hand on hip, a defiant stance, but he was not smiling. He stared at the camera with grim intensity. There was something sad about the eyes.

Behind him, quite clearly visible, stood his aircraft. There was no mistaking the lean, sleek silhouette of the Mosquito fighter-bomber, nor the two low-slung pods housing the twin Merlin engines that gave it its remarkable performance. I was about to say something to Joe when I felt a gust of cold air on my back. One of the windows had blown open and the icy air was rushing in.

'I'll close it, sir,' the old man said, and made to put all the plates back down again.

'No, I'll do it.'

It took me two strides to cross to where the window swung on its steel frame. To get a better hold, I stepped inside the curtain and stared out. The fog swirled in waves round the old mess building, disturbed by the current of warm air coming from the window. Somewhere, far away in the fog, I thought I heard the snarl of engines. There were no engines out there, just a motorcycle of some farm boy, taking leave of his sweetheart across the fens. I closed the window, made sure it was secure and turned back into the room.

'Who's the pilot, Joe?'

'The pilot, sir?'

I nodded towards the lonely photograph on the mantel.

'Oh, I see, sir. That's a photo of Mr John Kavanagh. He was here during the war, sir.'

He placed the wineglass on the topmost plate.

'Kavanagh?' I walked back to the picture and studied it closely.

'Yes, sir. An Irish gentleman. A very fine man, if I may say so. As a matter of fact, sir, this was his room.'

'What squadron was that, Joe?' I was still peering at the aircraft in the background.

'Pathfinders, sir. Mosquitos, they flew. Very fine pilots, all of them, sir. But I venture to say I believe Mr Johnny was the best of them all. But then I'm biased, sir. I was his batman, you see.'

There was no doubting it. The faint letters on the nose of the Mosquito behind the figure in the photo read JK. Not Jig King, but Johnny Kavanagh.

The whole thing was as clear as day. Kavanagh had been

a fine pilot, flying with one of the crack squadrons during the war. After the war he'd left the Air Force, probably going into second-hand car dealing, as quite a few did. So he'd made a pile of money in the booming Fifties, probably bought himself a fine country house, and had enough left over to indulge his real passion – flying. Or rather re-creating the past, his days of glory. He'd bought up an old Mosquito in one of the RAF periodic auctions of obsolescent aircraft, refitted it, and flew it privately whenever he wished. Not a bad way to spend your spare time, if you had the money.

So he'd been flying back from some trip to Europe, had spotted me turning in triangles above the cloud bank, realized I was stuck and taken me in tow. Pinpointing his position precisely by crossed radio beacons, knowing this stretch of the coast by heart, he'd taken a chance on finding his old airfield at Minton, even in thick fog. It was a hell of a risk. But then I had no fuel left, anyway, so it was that or bust.

I had no doubt I could trace the man, probably through the Royal Aero Club.

'He was certainly a good pilot,' I said reflectively, thinking of this evening's performance.

'The best, sir,' said old Joe from behind me. 'They reckoned he had eyes like a cat, did Mr Johnny. I remember many's the time the squadron would return from dropping marker flares over bombing targets in Germany and the rest of the young gentlemen would go into the bar and have a drink. More likely several.'

'He didn't drink?' I asked.

'Oh, yes, sir, but more often he'd have his Mosquito refuelled and take off again alone, going back over the Channel or the North Sea to see if he could find some crippled bomber making for the coast and guide it home.'

I frowned. The big bombers had their own bases to go to.

'But some of them would have taken a lot of enemy flak fire and sometimes they had their radios knocked out. All over, they came from. Marham, Scampton, Waddington; the big four-engined ones, Halifaxes, Stirlings, and Lancasters; a bit before your time, if you'll pardon my saying so, sir.'

'I've seen pictures of them,' I admitted. 'And some of them fly in air parades. And he used to guide them back?'

I could imagine them in my mind's eye, gaping holes in

the body, wings, and tail, creaking and swaying as the pilot sought to hold them steady for home, a wounded or dying crew and the radio shot to bits. And I knew, from too recent experience, the bitter loneliness of the winter's sky at night, with no radio, no guide for home, and the fog blotting out the land.

'That's right, sir. He used to go up for a second flight in the same night, patrolling out over the North Sea, looking for a crippled plane. Then he'd guide it home, back here to Minton, sometimes through fog so dense you couldn't see your hand. Sixth sense, they said he had – something of the Irish in him.'

I turned from the photograph and stubbed my cigarette butt into the ashtray by the bed. Joe was at the door.

'Quite a man,' I said, and I meant it. Even today, middle-aged, he was a superb flyer.

'Oh, yes, sir, quite a man, Mr Johnny. I remember him saying to me once, standing right where you are, before the fire: "Joe," he said, "whenever there's one of them out there in the night, trying to get back, I'll go out and bring him home."'

I nodded gravely. The old man so obviously worshipped his wartime officer.

'Well,' I said, 'by the look of it, he's still doing it.'

Now Joe smiled.

'Oh, I hardly think so, sir. Mr Johnny went out on his last patrol Christmas Eve 1943, just fourteen years ago tonight. He never came back, sir. He went down with his plane some-where out there in the North Sea. Good night, sir. And Happy Christmas.'

---

1   Divide into groups to complete either of the following
     projects:

1.1 Make a model or display to show what life was like on a
     Norfolk airfield in 1943, so as to explain the following
     elements of the story:

        accommodation for RAF personnel
        flying dress
        types of aircraft
        RAF bases in East Anglia
        crippled aircraft returning to base

There are many reference books available which give this information. Other novels are set against the same background, such as Len Deighton's *Bomber* and *Goodbye, Mickey Mouse*.

1.2 Forsyth has used a number of techniques to heighten feelings of suspense in the reading of the story:

> a drop in temperature ('. . . feeling the room suddenly go cold')
> description of characters ('. . . stared at the camera with grim intensity')
> suspense ('I felt the gust of cold wind on my back')
> coincidence ('This was his room . . . I was his batman . . . looking for a crippled plane . . . standing right where you are . . . fourteen years ago tonight')
> incongruity ('Happy Christmas')

Write some stories of your own using these techniques, so as to create feelings of suspense and mystery. They can be true stories you have heard, or ones which you have made up.

---

2   Answer the following questions:

2.1 What is the 'mantel' above the fire, where Johnny Kavanagh's photograph is to be seen?

2.2 Where are 'the fens' and what are they?

2.3 The normal life of the young RAF pilot is conveyed by his habits ('. . . cigarette half-raised to his lips . . . wineglass . . .'), his language ('It was a hell of a risk') and the way he thought of life ('Not a bad way to spend your time – if you had the money'). Which groups of religious people would say that he could not be a religious man on the basis of such a lifestyle? Why would they say this? What do you feel yourself?

2.4 Write sentences using the words 'defiant', 'grim', 'indulge', 'periodic', 'obsolescent'.

2.5 Why do some people like to read ghost stories at Christmas? (Dickens' *The Christmas Carol* is another Christmas ghost story.) Is it perhaps because it makes people get closer together around the fire and they feel their togetherness, or is it because it heightens the feeling of mystery in Christmas? Can you think of any other reasons?

3   Look back at the coincidences of the story which are listed
in question 1.2. What has happened is that Johnny
Kavanagh has broken through time. He is doing the same
thing in 1957 that he was doing in 1943. Now carefully
read the following stories and analyse what it is which has
broken down to make the events possible:

Some Christian missionaries were working in China during
the period when the Communist army was taking over the
country. Their flat-roofed home was surrounded by a wall on
a rise in the centre of a village – which was, itself, situated on
a hill. They knew that their work was finished because it
would be opposed by the new authorities, and all that they
might expect at the best was for their lives to be spared and
for them to be sent home.

All day the sounds of battle had come nearer and so, as
darkness fell, the missionaries met together in their home
and asked that God would protect them. During the night the
battle seemed to reach the village and then pass them by,
leaving them untouched and unharmed. In the morning an
army officer arrived by truck with a number of soldiers.

'Where are the soldiers who guarded this house last
night?' he demanded.

'What soldiers?' they replied.

'There were twelve soldiers clearly seen on the roof of
this house; they did not fire and so we passed the village by
and it is surrounded.'

The officer was taken to the roof . . . his men searched
the village . . . there were no soldiers, and no signs that
soldiers had ever been there. It was a mystery.

When they arrived back in England, the missionaries
were sent by their employing missionary society to take
meetings where they could explain about their work, and to
get increased financial support for their society. One of them
returned to his home church and told the story of the missing
soldiers.

'Exactly when was this?' asked the vicar.

Dates were compared.

'It was the night of the vestry prayer meeting,' he said
with increasing excitement. 'We all felt that we should
specially pray for your protection that night. There were
twelve of us.'

When the Jews were exiled to Babylon in the sixth century BC, the Babylonian king, Nebuchadnezzar, erected a golden statue that everyone was commanded to bow down to and worship. Three young Jews who served in the royal court refused to do this and they were denounced by enemies. The story of what happened is told in the Jewish sacred books and is recorded in the Bible, in the book of Daniel, chapter 3.

Furious with rage, Nebuchadnezzar summoned Shadrach, Meshach and Abednego. So these men were brought before the king, and Nebuchadnezzar said to them, 'Is it true, Shadrach, Meshach and Abednego, that you do not serve my gods or worship the image of gold I have set up? Now when you hear the sound of the horn, flute, zither, lyre, harp, pipes and all kinds of music, if you are ready to fall down and worship the image I made, very good. But if you do not worship it, you will be thrown immediately into a blazing furnace. Then what god will be able to rescue you from my hand?'

Shadrach, Meshach and Abednego replied to the king, 'O Nebuchadnezzar, we do not need to defend ourselves before you in this matter. If we are thrown into the blazing furnace, the God we serve is able to save us from it, and he will rescue us from your hand, O king. But even if he does not, we want you to know, O king, that we will not serve your gods, or worship the image of gold you have set up.'

Then Nebuchadnezzar was furious . . . and his attitude towards them changed. He ordered the furnace to be heated seven times hotter than usual and commanded some of his strongest soldiers to tie up Shadrach, Meshach and Abednego and throw them into the blazing furnace . . . The king's command was so urgent and the furnace was so hot that the flames of the fire killed the men who took up Shadrach, Meshach and Abednego, and these three men, firmly tied, fell into the blazing furnace.

Then King Nebuchadnezzar leaped to his feet in amazement and asked his advisers, 'Wasn't it three men that we tied up and threw into the fire?'

They replied, 'Certainly, O king.'

He said, 'Look! I see four men walking around in the fire, unbound and unharmed, and the fourth looks like a son of the gods.'

Nebuchadnezzar then approached the opening of the

blazing furnace and shouted, '. . . Come out. Come here!'

So Shadrach, Meshach and Abednego came out of the fire and the satraps, prefects, governors and royal advisers crowded round them. They saw that the fire had not harmed their bodies, nor was a hair of their head singed; their robes were not scorched, and there was no smell of fire on them.

There is a story in the New Testament which also tells about a rescue act. It is Acts, chapter 12:

It was about this time that King Herod arrested some who belonged to the church, intending to persecute them. He had James, the brother of John, put to death with the sword. When he saw that this pleased the Jews, he proceeded to seize Peter also. This happened during the feast of Unleavened Bread. After arresting him, he put him in prison, handing him over to be guarded by four squads of four soldiers each. Herod intended to bring him out for public trial after the Passover.

So Peter was kept in prison, but the church was earnestly praying to God for him.

The night before Herod was to bring him to trial, Peter was sleeping between two soldiers, bound with two chains, and sentries stood guard at the entrance. Suddenly an angel of the Lord appeared and a light shone in the cell. He struck Peter on the side and woke him up. 'Quick, get up!' he said, and the chains fell off Peter's wrists.

Then the angel said to him, 'Put on your clothes and sandals.' And Peter did so. 'Wrap your cloak around you and follow me,' the angel told him. Peter followed him out of prison, but he had no idea that what the angel was doing was really happening; he thought he was seeing a vision. They passed the first and second guards and came to the iron gate leading to the city. It opened for them by itself, and they went through it. When they had walked the length of the street, suddenly the angel left him.

Now answer the following questions, writing down the answers after you have discussed them as a group:

3.1 In which story is there a breakdown in the normal rules of space?

In which story is there a breakdown of normal physical properties?

In which story is there a breakdown of normal human faculties?

Are these the same kinds of breakdown, or are they different from the breakdown in time in the story of *The Shepherd*?

3.2 Are these kinds of things impossible, or is the way that we look at 'the laws of science' wrong?

Should science make room for things like this?

Is it true that science is limited to what it can observe in space and time, and that therefore such happenings as have been recorded in this section are outside the scope of science?

3.3 It has sometimes been said that although such happenings do not obey the laws of physical science, they do obey the higher laws of love. Was somebody helped or rescued when they needed it in each of these stories?

Do you think it is possible for love to break through the normal barriers of space and time?

3.4 What kind of person would see such events as evidence for a loving God?

How would an atheist respond to such stories?

✡ 9
WITCHCRAFT AND SUPERSTITION

Those who believe in a particular religion do not always agree about everything. Differences sometimes arise between Christians over how the Bible is to be understood. The people of the Bible seem to have believed that there is an unseen world of evil, spiritual powers under the control of a supreme evil spirit known as Satan or the devil. They believed that it was possible for some people to have contact with the spirit world and use its power. Such people were called witches or sorcerers. They also believed that it was possible for people to come under the power of the world of evil spiritual powers. Such people were said to be 'possessed' by evil spirits.

It will be helpful at this point to look up the following references in the Bible as examples of the kind of stories which reflect this belief:

Witches and sorcerers: 1 Samuel chapter 28, verses 3–25; Acts 13:1–12
Spirit possession: Mark 1:21–28; 5:1–20; 9:14–29
Protection for Christians: Mark 16:16–18

In the twentieth century, some Christians believe that all the Bible is doing is teaching us about the superstitions of the past and they therefore dismiss any talk about witches or evil spirits today. Other Christians believe that the same powers operate in the twentieth century world, and that the Bible gives us help to know how to deal with such evil powers, and instructions to avoid the occult.

Four hundred years ago, the Puritans took biblical passages such as Exodus 22:18 and Deuteronomy 18:9–13 very seriously and literally, so as to kill people they believed to be witches.

Pendle Hill in Lancashire has always been associated with witches. In *Mist over Pendle* Robert Neill tells how Margery was sent to Pendle from London when her parents died; she went to live with her cousin, Roger Nowell, who was a landowner and the local magistrate. Margery soon learned about the local witches who were said to be able to curse people so that they died, and she caught the reaction of the Puritan country folk, such as Richard Baldwin, who feared them. One day she rode with her cousin to the local mill to find that one of the local witches had been caught, tied up, and was about to be 'swum' in the mill pond . . .

Robert Neill
Mist Over
Pendle

Here all was familiar, and today so strange. For round the pool that was always so quiet and lonely, there was now a swaying surging rabble, perhaps a hundred of them – men and women, and even some children too. They were all wet, all cold, and all ripe for mischief. In the centre of them the press was thinner and here, bare-headed and commanding, was Richard Baldwin.

The crowd turned as they heard the horses, and those on the fringe pressed back in alarm, leaving a lane into which Roger promptly rode. He was not gentle; he forced his way ruthlessly; but he got through; and Margery, who had kept close, dismounted at his side, watchful and anxious.

Richard Baldwin, tight-lipped and stern, stood by the low stone wall and waited silently for Roger. At his side was a man whom Margery did not know, a chubby fresh-complexioned fellow with the clothes and air of a townsman; at another time he might have looked genial, but now, with his round face puckered, his podgy chin set tight, and his clothes soaked through with rain and mud, he had all the look of an angry and dangerous man. But Margery spared him no more than a glance, for behind him, on the ground, was Alizon Device; and Alizon Device was ready to be swum. She lay naked in the mud, scratched, bruised and bleeding, with the cold rain splashing on her. Her left wrist was tied to her right ankle and her right wrist to her left ankle, and her rolling eyes and twitching lips showed the extremity of her terror. Standing behind her, muddy and dishevelled, was Harry Hargreaves, and he greeted Roger with unconcealed relief.

Roger nodded to him and turned sharply to Margery.

'Untie that girl,' he said curtly.

Richard Baldwin moved forward quickly, his face set and hard.

'Master Nowell . . .'

'Go to your homes – each one of you, and at once.' Roger's voice went sharply to the crowd, and Baldwin waited. Margery, tense and breathless, heard a stir and a buzz – and that was all. None moved. And Richard Baldwin spoke again.

'You'd best know . . .'

'I mean to know.'

Roger snapped it, and the crackle in his voice won him silence. He glanced sharply at Margery, and she hastily remembered what he had told her to do; at once she pulled the gloves from her frozen fingers and dropped on her knees by the writhing Alizon. Then a fierce hand clapped on her shoulder, and the chubby-faced stranger spun her round and spoke angrily.

'You'll leave that . . .'

He got no further. Roger's sword was out like a striking snake, and the point pricked blood from the fellow's throat. He jumped like a startled goat, and at once Roger was between him and Margery.

'Do you stay your hands, or do I slit your throat?'

It was enough. The fellow pressed back, not a word said, against the wall of the pool; and again Margery knelt and fumbled with the knots in the tough wet cord.

---

1 Answer the following questions about the extract from *Mist Over Pendle*:

1.1 What is meant by:
'tight-lipped'
'fresh-complexioned'
'puckered'
'podgy'
'dishevelled'

1.2 What was it that excited the 'swaying, surging rabble'? Was it enthusiasm for God's work, or was there something else involved? What might this tell us about some forms of religious enthusiasm?

1.3 How was a witch 'swum'? What other means did people use during this period to prove whether or not a person was a witch? What would have happened if Alizon had floated, which justified the magistrate's action?

1.4 Why was it that old ladies, who often lived alone, were thought to be witches?

2   Go back to the stories from the Bible which are referred to
in the references at the beginning of the chapter and then
answer the following questions:

2.1 Why did King Saul think that the spirit of a dead person
might be able to help him?

2.2 What do you think actually happened in the home of the
witch (or medium) of En-Dor?

2.3 In what ways is the story similar to and different from what
happens at a Spiritualist seance?

2.4 Why would a Roman governor employ a sorcerer?

2.5 What means do people use in the twentieth century to try
to get the kind of information which was gained from a
sorcerer?

2.6 Do you think that people can be affected by evil spirits?

2.7 What kind of power did Jesus have which gave him the
ability to exorcise evil spirits?

2.8 Have you ever heard of twentieth century Christians using
the kind of protection which is promised in Mark 16? Write
an account of such an example when you have found one.

2.9 Do you think it is important or unimportant that Christians
differ on whether or not there are evil spirits?

2.10 Do you think that it is 'asking for trouble' to get involved
with the occult?

3   Find out all that you can about Hallowe'en, so as to 'read a
paper' to other members of your group. In preparing your
paper, you should consider the following:

●In pagan times, 31 October was the eve of the New
Year, and it was believed that witches and spirits were
active. Great fires were lit to ensure renewal of life after
the great sleep (or death) of winter.
●The early Christians felt they could not break this
custom, so used it to get Christians to remember the
saints who were already dead. Hallowe'en is therefore
followed by All Saints Day.
●Hallowe'en is often celebrated with decorations,
parties, mischief and ancient customs. It often forms the
basis of work in schools. One teachers' association
believes that this is harmful and dangerous.
●In the USA it is illegal in some schools for children
to learn anything about Easter or Christmas because

these are 'religious' and religion may not be taught in schools; but, theoretically at least, they can learn about witchcraft, evil spirits and Hallowe'en because these are not religious! Is this dangerous?

Consider the following account which was written by a head of house in a comprehensive school in the UK. He was a Christian.

Two prefects came to the staff room door during the dinner hour.

'Sir, please can you come and help. One of the fourth year girls in the house seems to be ill and is asking for you in the library.'

[1]Mary is not her real name, but every other detail in the story is true

I went to the library to find Mary[1] crouching in a corner on the floor, her face grey with fear. At first she couldn't speak to me, but after a few minutes, when everyone had been cleared from the library by the prefects, she sat at a table and told me her story. The night before, she said, she had been to a party, and towards the end of the evening one of the girls got out a ouija board 'to have a bit of fun'. They made a circle and put their hands on a glass, asking the spirit of the glass to spell out messages for them as it moved from letter to letter on the board.

At first it seemed a bit scary but pretty harmless until the glass began to move and to spell out a long message. It was for her. It said that six things would happen to her in order; and then she would die. During the day five of the things had happened. She was waiting for the sixth and then she would die.

I knew that Mary was a member of the school's Christian Union, and that she was a member of the RE set for examinations, so I asked her if she was a Christian. When she told me, 'Yes', I asked her if she didn't know that the Bible says we should not get involved with the world of spirits. She hadn't realized this. I then asked her if she believed that Jesus had the same power today as he did in his lifetime to overcome the spirit world. She said that she did.

So because I knew she was a Christian and was a Christian myself, I said a simple prayer, asking for forgiveness for her that she had got involved with the occult, and asking Jesus to break the evil power which had control of her.

When she opened her eyes, the fear had gone. I got the

prefects to make her a strong cup of tea in their common room and she got over it completely.

I am quite sure that something serious could have happened. She was so taken up by the suggestion made by the ouija board that she believed she was going to die, and she could have frightened herself to death.

Discuss this incident in a group and bring out these points:

- what is meant by 'the power of suggestion'
- whether you feel that someone at the party was playing around with the glass or whether the spirit world was really involved
- whether it ultimately made any difference to Mary whether it was spirit-real or not
- whether or not you think the head of house was naïve
- the function of the teacher's prayer if someone had simply been playing around, and the function of the prayer if the spirit world was really involved
- how you would advise a friend who told you that they were going to a party where they would be playing with an ouija board, tarot cards, fortune telling and so on
- how you would help someone who had been badly frightened by the occult world

☆ 10
PREJUDICE

In the second half of the eighteenth century, Arabs and Europeans raided the villages of West Africa to find strong men who could be sold as slaves to the plantation owners in America and in the West Indies. Kunta Kinte was an African who was taken in this way, and six generations later a journalist-descendent describes conditions on the slave ship before his ancestor was sold to a plantation owner in Virginia:

Alex Haley
Roots

Kunta wondered if he had gone mad. Naked, chained, shackled, he awoke on his back between two other men in a pitch darkness full of steamy heat and sickening stink and a nightmarish bedlam of shrieking, weeping, praying, and vomiting. He could feel and smell his own vomit on his chest and belly. His whole body was one spasm of pain from the beatings he had received in the four days since his capture. But the place where the hot iron had been put between his shoulders hurt the worst.

A rat's thick, furry body brushed his cheek, its whiskered nose sniffing at his mouth. Quivering with revulsion, Kunta snapped his teeth together desperately, and the rat ran away. In rage, Kunta snatched and kicked against the shackles that bound his wrists and ankles. Instantly, angry exclamations and jerking came back from whomever he was shackled to. The shock and pain adding to his fury, Kunta lunged upward, his head bumping hard against wood – right on the spot where he had been clubbed by the toubob back in the woods. Gasping and snarling, he and the unseen man next to him battered their iron cuffs at each other until both slumped back in exhaustion. Kunta felt himself starting to vomit again, and he tried to force it back, but couldn't. His already emptied belly squeezed up a thin, sour fluid that drained from the side of his mouth as he lay wishing that he might die.

He told himself that he mustn't lose control again if he wanted to save his strength and his sanity. After a while, when he felt he could move again, he very slowly and carefully explored his shackled right wrist and ankle with his left hand. They were bleeding. He pulled lightly on the chain; it seemed to be connected to the left ankle and wrist of the man he had fought with. On Kunta's left, chained to him by the ankles, lay some other man, someone who kept up a steady moaning, and they were all so close that their shoulders, arms, and legs touched if any of them moved even a little.

Remembering the wood he had bumped into with his head, Kunta drew himself upward again, just enough for it to bump gently; there wasn't enough space even to sit up. And behind his head was a wooden wall. I'm trapped like a leopard in a snare, he thought. Then he remembered sitting in the darkness of the manhood-training hut after being taken blindfolded to the jujuo so many rains before, and a sob welled up in his throat; but he fought it back. Kunta made himself think about the cries and groans he was hearing all around him. There must be many men here in the blackness, some close, some farther away, some beside him, others in front of him, but all in one room, if that's what this was. Straining his ears, he could hear still more cries, but they were muffled and came from below, beneath the splintery planking he lay on.

Listening more intently, he began to recognise the different tongues of those around him. Over and over, in Arabic, a Fulani was shouting, 'Allah in heaven, help me!' And a man of the Serere tribe was hoarsely wailing what must have been the names of his family. But mostly Kunta heard Mandinkas, the loudest of them babbling wildly in the sira kango secret talk of men, vowing terrible deaths to all toubob. The cries of the others were so slurred with weeping that Kunta could identify neither their words nor their languages, although he knew that some of the strange talk he heard must come from beyond The Gambia.

As Kunta lay listening, he slowly began to realize that he was trying to push from his mind the impulse to relieve the demands of his bowels, which he had been forcing back for days. But he could hold it in no longer, and finally the faeces curled out between his buttocks. Revolted at himself, smelling his own addition to the stench, Kunta began sobbing, and again his belly spasmed, producing this time only a little spittle; but he kept gagging. What sins was he being punished for in such a manner as this? He pleaded to Allah for an answer. It was sin enough that he hadn't prayed once since the morning he went for the wood to make his drum. Though he couldn't get onto his knees, and he knew not even which way was east, he closed his eyes where he lay and prayed, beseeching Allah's forgiveness.

Nearly two hundred years later, slavery had been abolished in the United States of America, but the descendants of the slaves suffered great discrimination. One of the worst areas was in getting justice.

The kind of thing which could happen is brought out by Harper Lee when he tells how Tom Robinson, a black American, was falsely accused of raping a white woman. He was defended by Atticus, the local lawyer, who clearly exposed the false nature of the charge.

In this extract from the story, the lawyer's little daughter, Jean Louise, recalls how the jury reached their verdict:

Harper Lee
To Kill a
Mockingbird

Mr Tate said, 'This court will come to order,' in a voice that rang with authority, and the heads below us jerked up. Mr Tate left the room and returned with Tom Robinson. He steered Tom to his place beside Atticus, and stood there. Judge Taylor had roused himself to sudden alertness and was sitting up straight, looking at the empty jury box.

What happened after that had a dreamlike quality: in a dream I saw the jury return, moving like underwater swimmers, and Judge Taylor's voice came from far away, and was tiny. I saw something only a lawyer's child could be expected to see, could be expected to watch for, and it was like watching Atticus walk into the street, raise a rifle to his shoulder and pull the trigger, but watching all the time knowing that the gun was empty.

A jury never looks at a defendant it has convicted, and when this jury came in, not one of them looked at Tom Robinson. The foreman handed a piece of paper to Mr Tate who handed it to the clerk who handed it to the judge . . .

I shut my eyes. Judge Taylor was polling the jury: 'Guilty

... guilty ... guilty ... guilty ...' I peeked at Jem: his hands were white from gripping the balcony rail, and his shoulders jerked as if each 'guilty' was a separate stab between them.

Judge Taylor was saying something. His gavel was in his fist, but he wasn't using it. Dimly, I saw Atticus pushing papers from the table into his brief-case. He snapped it shut, went to the court reporter and said something, nodded to Mr Gilmer, and then went to Tom Robinson and whispered something to him. Atticus put his hand on Tom's shoulder as he whispered. Atticus took his coat off the back of his chair and pulled it over his shoulder. Then he left the court-room, but not by his usual exit. He must have wanted to go home the short way, because he walked quickly down the middle aisle towards the south exit. I followed the top of his head as he made his way to the door. He did not look up.

Someone was punching me, but I was reluctant to take my eyes from the people below us, and from the image of Atticus's lonely walk down the aisle.

'Miss Jean Louise?'

I looked around. They were standing. All around us and in the balcony on the opposite wall, the Negroes were getting to their feet. Reverend Sykes's voice was as distant as Judge Taylor's:

'Miss Jean Louise, stand up. Your father's passin'.'

---

1 Write sentences using words opposite in meaning to the following:

pitch darkness	jerked up
furry	authority
slumped back	whispered
steady moaning	reluctant
splintery	
slurred	

---

2 From the context, explain the meaning and significance of the following words:

toubob	foreman
jujuo	gavel
rains	
Allah	
Mandinkas	

3   Undertake one of the following extended pieces of work:

3.1 Using any other resources you can find, write an account of the slave trade between Europe, Africa and America. Include in your account an explanation of how it ended and people who were involved in the abolition.

3.2 Using any other resources you can find, write an account of the struggle for freedom and equality by black people. Include in your account what is happening at the present time and some of the people who are involved.

3.3 Write an account of any of the advanced central African or west African civilizations which are known from ancient times.

4   Answer the following questions carefully:

4.1 How would Kunta have prayed, as a Muslim, had he not been lying on his back in a slave ship, chained to two other men?

4.2 What references in the extract from *Roots* show that the Europeans treated the Africans like animals?

4.3 How is the prejudice towards black people in the United States of the 1930s (exemplified in *To Kill a Mockingbird*) based upon treatment of black people in the 1760s (exemplified in *Roots*)?

4.4 What did Jean Louise mean when she said, 'It was like watching Atticus walk into the street, raise a rifle to his shoulder and pull the trigger, but watching all the time knowing that the gun was empty'? Why did she feel like this?

4.5 Read the following passages in the Bible, found in the New Testament: Ephesians chapter 6, verses 5–6; Colossians 3:22–24; Luke 22:24–27; Galatians 3:26–27; 1 John 3: 16–18. Do you agree with the view that although the Christians of the first century CE did not try to abolish slavery at a time when it was a normal feature of life, they instituted teaching which would one day make all people free?

5

Insert the following words in the correct places in the gaps in the passage which follows:

arson	graffiti	prejudice
cultures	history	racism
curious	insecure	school
discrimination	insulting	security
employment	language	threat
foolish	negative	tokenism
God	physically	weak

RACISM

The human being has many needs. When needs of food and shelter are met we grow _____, but we also have needs which have to be met for us to grow as persons.

One such need is security. If we feel threatened and _____, we fail to grow up into a person who can cope. The things we are used to in our upbringing and culture provide security. They provide some kind of reference-point from which we can build our lives. If our culture is threatened we lose our _____.

One of the most common threats to our security is the presence of people from other _____. When other people look different, speak a different _____, raise their families differently, worship _____ in another way and have different customs and _____, it puts the importance of our own culture in doubt and we feel threatened and insecure.

If we are strong enough to do things we may therefore act so as to keep people from the other culture at a distance, keep them weak, believe that they are _____ or even seek to destroy them. All of these actions are forms of racism.

Prejudice is a form of _____. Prejudice means pre-judging someone; giving an opinion before one knows the whole truth of the matter. In racism, it is always a _____ form of prejudice, such as 'all blacks are dirty' or 'no whites are to be trusted'. The _____ sometimes results in _____ words like 'wogs' or 'wasps' and in insulting jokes about races. It gives rise to stereotypes about races. (ALL Africans are primitive, or ALL Englishmen wear bowler hats and carry umbrellas.) It leads to attitudes in which we treat people as _____ or quaint, as though they were objects of interest to be observed, and to _____,

which is an acknowledgment that some parts of the
other culture have some value. Prejudice stays just so long
as the rival culture is of little threat, but as soon as the rival
culture becomes a _____, prejudice takes more
active forms to ensure that it stays weak.

_____ is action taken to deny people the same
opportunities as the stronger group. It may involve losing
opportunities to vote in elections, to travel on buses or even
to attend _____. It can deny access to housing
and _____. Discrimination is often hidden, but if it
is ineffective, the opposition may come out into the open in
various violent forms of action designed to make members
of the rival culture feel afraid and therefore _____.
This may be in verbal form as when _____
appears on walls, but it may also involve physical violence,
_____ and mass killing.

Racism will only finally be overcome when people have
such inner security that they do not need to take action
against those they feel threaten them from another culture.

---

6   In the light of what you have learned about racism through
the previous exercise, read and comment upon the
following poem, which was written by a Welshman about
the attitudes of the English towards them:

R. S. Thomas   A WELSH TESTAMENT
in *Tares*

All right, I was Welsh. Does it matter?
I spoke a tongue that was passed on
To me in the place I happened to be,
A place huddled between grey walls
Of cloud for at least half the year.
My word for heaven was not yours.

The word for hell had a sharp edge
Put on it by the hand of the wind
Honing, honing with a shrill sound
Day and night. Nothing that Glyn Dwr
Knew was armour against the rain's
Missiles. What was descent from him?

Even God had a Welsh name:
He spoke to him in the old language;

He was to have a peculiar care
For the Welsh people. History showed us
He was too big to be nailed to a wall
Of a stone chapel, yet still we crammed him
Between the boards of a black book.

Yet men sought us despite this.
My high cheek-bones, my length of skull
Drew them as to a rare portrait
By a dead master. I saw them stare
From their long cars, as I passed knee deep
In ewes and ethers. I saw them stand
By the thorn hedges, watching me string
The far flocks on a shrill whistle.
And always there were their eyes' strong
Pressure on me: You are Welsh, they said;
Speak to us so: keep your fields free
Of the smell of petrol, the loud roar
Of hot tractors; we must have peace
And quietness.

      Is a museum
Peace? I asked. Am I the keeper
Of the heart's relics, blowing the dust
In my own eyes? I am a man;
I never wanted the drab role
Life assigned me, an actor playing
To the past's audience upon a stage
Of earth and stone; the absurd label
Of birth, or race hanging askew
About my shoulders. I was in prison
Until you came; your voice was a key
Turning in the enormous lock
Of hopelessness. Did the door open
To let me out or yourselves in?

11
SUFFERING

During the 1939–45 World War, six-and-a-half million Jews were put to death in Europe. The National Socialist (Nazi) party which had taken over Germany looked upon Jews as the cause of every possible problem, and pursued a policy of extermination. As the German armies conquered Europe, Jews were rounded up from their homes and taken away to camps where they were put to death, and their bodies burned or buried.

Not all Germans knew about it, and some tried to help the Jewish people. Otto Schindler was a wealthy German industrialist who used his factory to save the lives of many Jews in Poland by making sure that they were employed there. The factory became known as 'Schindler's Ark' and the story is told by Thomas Keneally who wrote a book with that title.

In the book, Keneally describes how Schindler first discovered what was going on by listening to Bachner, a young pharmacist from Cracow who had escaped from the death camp at Belzec . . .

Thomas
Keneally
Schindler's Ark

[1]The Ukraine is an area now incorporated into the Soviet Union at its border with Europe

[2]The SS were German intelligence officers

. . . He had seen the final horror, he said. He was mad-eyed and his hair had silvered in his brief absence. All the Cracow people who had been rounded up in early June had been taken nearly to Russia, he said, to the camp of Belzec. When the trains arrived at the railway station the people were driven out by Ukrainians[1] with clubs. There was a frightful stench about the place, but an SS man[2] had kindly told people that that was due to the use of disinfectant. The people were lined up in front of two large warehouses, one marked 'Cloak Room' and the other 'Valuables'. The new arrivals were made to undress and a small Jewish boy passed among the crowd handing out lengths of string with which to tie their shoes together. Spectacles and rings were removed. So, naked, the prisoners had their heads shaved in the hairdressers', an SS NCO[3] telling them that their hair was needed to make something special for U-boat[4] crews. It would grow again, he said, maintaining the myth of their continued usefulness. At last the victims were driven down a barbed-wire corridor to bunkers which had copper Stars of David on their roofs and were labelled 'Baths and Inhalation Rooms'. SS men reassured them all the way, telling them to breathe deeply, that it was an excellent means of disinfection. Bachner saw a little girl drop a bracelet on the ground, and a boy of three picked it up and went into the bunker playing with it.

In the bunkers, said Bachner, they were all gassed. And afterwards squads were sent in to disentangle the pyramid of corpses and take the bodies away for burial. It had taken barely two days, he said, before they were all dead, except for him. While waiting in a great enclosure for his turn, he'd become alarmed by the tone of the reassurances issuing from the SS and, somehow getting to a latrine, had lowered himself into the pit. He'd stayed there three days, the human waste up to his neck. His face, he said, had been a hive of flies. He'd slept standing, wedged in the hole for fear of drowning there. At last he'd crawled out at night.

Somehow he'd walked out of Belzec, following the railway line. Everyone understood that he had got out precisely because he was beyond reason. He'd been cleaned by someone's hand – a peasant woman's perhaps – and put into fresh clothes for his journey back to the starting point . . .

The chambers of Belzec, Herr Schindler found out from his sources, had been completed by March that year under the supervision of a Hamburg engineering firm and of SS engineers from Oranienburg. From Bachner's testimony, it seemed that three thousand killings a day were not beyond their capacity. Crematoria were under construction, lest old fashioned means of disposal of corpses should put a brake on the new killing method. The same company involved in Belzec had installed identical facilities at Sobibor, also in the Lublin district. Bids had been accepted and construction was well advanced for a similar installation at Treblinka near Warsaw.

[3]Non-commissioned officer

[4]U-boats were submarines

1
The description of·Belzec is full of horror. The author adds to the horror in a number of ways. Describe what Keneally has done to increase the sense of shock and horror in the following phrases:

'. . . his hair had silvered in his brief absence.'
'. . . maintaining the myth of their continued usefulness.'
'. . . a boy of three picked it up and went into the bunker playing with it.'
'His face, he said, had been a hive of flies.'
'. . . completed by March that year under the supervision of a Hamburg engineering firm.'

Do you think it is right that authors should try to bring home to us the horror of things which happened nearly fifty years ago, or should it be forgotten? Discuss this in a group, and then summarize the reasons for the answer you would give.

2
Other books have been written against the background of the extermination of the Jewish people in Europe. Borrow one of the following from the library.

Ian Serallier, *The Silver Sword* (set in Poland)
The Diary of Anne Frank (set in Holland)
Corrie Ten Boom, *The Hiding Place* (set in Holland)
Ruth Dobschiner, *Selected to Live* (set in Holland)

3
Many Jews have said that Germany was a Christian country and therefore it was Christians who did this to them. They see this as the worst and most recent example of the hatred of Christians for Jews.

Jews came to England with William the Conqueror and Jewish communities grew up in London, Exeter, Bury St Edmunds, York and Norwich. They were mostly traders, doctors and money-lenders. They were not liked by poor people who too easily thought of them as 'murderers of Jesus' and they were disliked by the wealthy because they lent money at interest.

After a riot in London in 1204 King John found it necessary to make an order protecting the Jews because they were his subjects and therefore 'belonged' to him. The order said:

'We say this for our Jews and for our peace, that if we have granted our peace to anyone it shall be observed inviolably. Henceforth however, we commit the Jews residing in the City of London to your custody, so that if any attempt to do them harm, you (the barons and magistrates) may defend them, coming to their assistance with an armed force.'

When the barons revolted against the king in 1215, they sacked the Jewish quarter in London and killed many Jews. In the rebellion of 1264 they massacred some 1500 Jews in London, and others in Canterbury and Northampton. In 1290, 16,000 Jews were expelled from England and they were not allowed to return until the time of Oliver Cromwell.

If you were a Christian and wanted to defend your faith against the points made above by Jewish people, how would you reply? The following questions are given to help you:

3.1 Is it true that *all* Christians have hated Jews?
Who was it who looked after Jews in *Selected to Live* (see 2, above)?
Why did people in Cromwell's time want Jews to return to England?
How did the British Government play a part in the return of the Jews to Israel in modern times?

3.2 Has there ever been a time when Jews persecuted Christians? In 135 CE, the Jews revolted against the Romans who occupied their country. Rabbi Akiva who led the revolt said that Bar Cochba, the Jewish general, was the Messiah. Christians who believed that Jesus was the Messiah would not fight under Bar Cochba. When the revolt was crushed, the Jews turned on the Christians for being traitors. No-one was to have anything to do with the Christians.

3.3 What do Christians and Jews have in common, and what are the main differences between them?

3.4 What is really meant by the term 'Christian'?
Is a Christian simply someone who lives in a traditionally Christian country; or someone who believes that Jesus really existed; or someone who believes that Christ's teachings are important; or someone who tries to follow his teaching; or someone who, because they believe Jesus to be spiritually alive today, can be forgiven for their wrong-doing and live their life with his help?
How might these very different ways of describing a Christian be used to explain things to a Jew?

3.5 Was Jesus a Jew? What evidence is there in the Christian New Testament that he was a Jew?

4   Answer one of the following questions:

4.1 If you were a deeply religious Jew who believed that God
had chosen the Jewish people and that they were therefore
in God's care, how would you try to explain the fact
that God had apparently let over six million Jews be
exterminated in Europe during World War II? (You might
want to ask a Jewish rabbi to help you understand this.)

4.2 If there is a God who Christians claim is a loving God, how
would you try to explain the fact that there is so much
suffering in the world – including the Holocaust (the name
given to the slaughter of the Jews in Europe)? When you
have thought out some of your answers, read the following
anonymous article, which was found in a church magazine.
What answer is it giving?

THE LONG SILENCE

At the end of time, billions of people were scattered on a
great plain before God's throne. Most shrank back from the
brilliant light before them. But some groups near the front
talked heatedly – not with cringing shame, but with
belligerence.

'Can God judge us? How can he know about suffering?'
snapped a pert young brunette. She ripped open a sleeve to
reveal a tattooed number from a Nazi concentration camp.
'We endured terror . . . beatings . . . torture . . . death!' In
another group a negro boy lowered his collar. 'What about
this?' he demanded, showing an ugly rope burn. 'Lynched for
no crime but being black!' In another crowd, a pregnant
schoolgirl with sullen eyes. 'Why should I suffer?' she
murmured. 'It wasn't my fault.'

Far out across the plain were hundreds of such groups.
Each had a complaint against God for the evil and suffering
permitted in his world. How lucky God was to live in heaven
where all was sweetness and light, where there was no weeping or fear, no hunger nor hatred. What did God know of all
that men had been forced to endure in this world? For God
lives a pretty sheltered life, they said.

So each of these groups sent forth their leader, chosen
because he had suffered the most. A Jew, a negro, a person
from Hiroshima, a horribly deformed arthritic, a thalidomide
child. In the centre of the plain they consulted with each

other. At last they were ready to present their case. It was rather clever.

Before God could be qualified to be their judge, he must endure what they endured. Their decision was that God should be sentenced to live on earth – as a man! Let him be born a Jew. Let the legitimacy of his birth be doubted! Give him a work so difficult that even his family will think him out of his mind when he tries to do it. Let him be betrayed by his closest friends. Let him face false charges, be tried by a prejudiced jury and convicted by a cowardly judge. Let him be tortured. At the last, let him see what it is to be terribly alone. Then let him die. Let him die so there can be no doubt he died. Let there be a great host of witnesses to verify it.

As each leader announced his portion of the sentence, loud murmurs of approval went up from the throng of people assembled. When the last had finished pronouncing sentence there was a long silence. No-one uttered another word. No-one moved.

For suddenly all knew that *God had already served his sentence*.

5

Judaism is a religion which is distinct from all other religions and has truth claims of its own. Christianity is also a religion which is distinct from all other religions and has truth claims of its own. Do you therefore think that people from different faiths can ever agree, or must religions always be in conflict?

Read the following children's poem:

John Godfrey Saxe 'The Blind Men and the Elephant' in *The Book of a Thousand Poems*

It was six men of Hindustan
To learning much inclined
Who went to see the elephant
(Though all of them were blind)
That each by observation
Might satisfy his mind.

The first approached the elephant
And happening to fall
Against his broad and sturdy side
At once began to bawl,
'Bless me, it seems the elephant
Is very like a wall.'

The second feeling of his tusk
Cried, 'Ho! What have we here?
So very round and smooth and strong
To me 'tis mighty clear
This wonder of an elephant
Is very like a spear.'

The third approached the animal
And happening to take
The squirming trunk within his hands
Then boldly up and spake.
'I see,' quoth he, 'the elephant
Is very like a snake.'

The fourth stretched out his eager hand
And felt about the knee,
'What most this mighty beast is like
Is very plain,' quoth he:
''Tis clear enough, the elephant
Is very like a tree.'

The fifth who chanced to touch the ear
Said 'Ev'n the blindest man
Can tell what this resembles most,
Deny the fact who can;
This marvel of an elephant is very like a fan.'

The sixth no sooner had begun
Around the beast to grope
Than, seizing on the swinging tail
That fell within his scope,
'I see,' cried he, 'the elephant
Is very like a rope.'

And so those men of Hindustan
Disputed loud and long
Each in his own opinion
Exceeding stiff and strong;
Though each was partly in the right
And all were in the wrong!

What was the author of the poem trying to say about
different beliefs?
Who might agree with him?
In what ways has he misunderstood the nature of religion?

☆ 12
☆ DEATH AND BEYOND

Members of some Indian tribes in North America believe that when a person hears an owl call his name, he is soon to die. *I Heard the Owl Call My Name* tells the story of Mark, a young Anglican clergyman, sent to serve in the Indian village of Kingcome in British Columbia. Unknown to him, he has only two years to live, but his bishop believes that the experience of living and working with the Indian people will be the most rewarding experience of his life. As the two years draw to a close, Mark is returning to the village in his boat and has a premonition that he is soon to die:

Margaret
Craven
*I Heard the Owl
Call My Name*

All day long he moved down the longest, and loveliest of all the inlets, and it seemed to him that something strange had happened to time. When he had first come to the village, it was the future that loomed huge. So much to plan. So much to learn. Then it was the present that had consumed him – each day with all its chores and never enough hours to do them. Now time had lost its contours. He seemed to see it as the raven or the bald eagle, flying high over the village, must see the part of the river that had passed the village, that had not yet reached the village, one and the same.

All day long, on his way back to Kingcome, because he was alone and receptive, the little questions, the observations he had pushed deep within him, began to rise slowly towards the door of the conscious mind which was almost ready to open, to receive them, and give them words: 'You are tired. You have told yourself that it was due to the winter which was hard on everyone. Deep inside haven't you known it was more than this? When the Bishop came to the potlatch and lingered after the others had gone, and went into the church by himself, didn't you guess then it had something to do with you? And your sister? When you took the boys down and lunched with her, did you not see the sadness in her eyes? And in the hospital, don't you remember the doctor's face, the look of quiet resignation upon it, and the way he hesitated an instant before answering your questions? And when the Bishop told you of the village, how carefully he did so. Did you not think, 'He is anxious I go there. Why?'

It was dusk when he entered Kingcome Inlet and moored the boat at the float, and climbed into the speedboat. When he entered the river, the stars were shining, the moon bright also, and he went slowly.

Soon the huge flights of snow geese would fly over the river on their way back to the nesting place, the spring swimmer would come up the river to the Clearwater, and on the river pairs of cocky, small, red-necked saw-bills would rest, the father flying off when Mark passed and the mother pretending she had broken a wing to lead him away from her little ones. And each would feel the pull of the earth and know his small place upon it, as did the Indian in his village.

He went slowly up the river. In front of the vicarage he anchored the boat and waded ashore. He trudged up the black sands to the path and stopped. From the dark spruce he heard an owl call – once, and again – and the questions that had been rising all day long reached the door of his mind and opened it.

He went up the path and the steps, through the living room and into the kitchen. The lights were on. At the stove Marta was preparing his dinner.

'Marta, something strange happened tonight. On the bank of the river I heard the owl call my name, and it was a question he asked, an answer he sought.'

She did not say, 'Nonsense, it was my name the owl called, and I am old and with me it does not matter.' She did not say, 'It's true you're thin and white, but who is not? It has no importance.'

She turned, spoon still in her hand, lifting her sweet, kind face with its network of tiny wrinkles, and she answered his question as she would have answered any other.

She said, 'Yes, my son.'

1   Answer the following questions:

    1.1 How does Margaret Craven in her story bring out the
following beliefs people have about approaching death?

        ● the loss of sense of time
        ● seeing significance in other people's reactions
        ● intensity of feelings about beauty and nature

    1.2 Do you think people have premonitions that they are going
to die?

    1.3 What do you think happens to a person when they die?
Talk this through as a group and then summarize the main
points made by the group.

2   We are all familiar with stories of people who have 'died'
and then have been restored to life by quick action on
the part of a doctor. Dr Raymond Moody studied the
experiences of over a hundred people who had this
happen to them, and found that their experiences were
remarkably similar. He records the results in his book,
Life After Life. He summarizes the kind of experiences
which such people go through:

Dr Raymond
Moody
Life After Life

A man is dying and, as he reaches the point of greatest
physical distress, he hears himself pronounced dead by his
doctor. He begins to hear an uncomfortable noise, a loud
ringing or buzzing, and at the same time feels himself moving
very rapidly through a long dark tunnel. After this, he suddenly finds himself outside of his own physical body, but still
in the immediate physical environment, and he sees his own
body from a distance, as though he is a spectator. He watches
the resuscitation attempt from this unusual vantage point
and is in a state of emotional upheaval.

After a while, he collects himself and becomes more
accustomed to his odd condition. He notices that he still has a
'body', but one of a very different nature and with very
different powers from the physical body he has left behind.
Soon other things begin to happen. Others come to meet and
to help him. He glimpses the spirits of relatives and friends
who have already died, and a loving, warm spirit of a kind he
has never encountered before – a being of light – appears
before him. This being asks him a question, nonverbally, to
make him evaluate his life and helps him along by showing

him a panoramic, instantaneous playback of the major events
of his life. At some point he finds himself approaching some
sort of barrier or border, apparently representing the limit
between earthly life and the next life. Yet, he finds that he
must go back to the earth, that the time for his death has
not yet come. At this point he resists, for by now he is taken
up with his experiences in the afterlife and does not want
to return. He is overwhelmed by intense feelings of joy,
love, and peace. Despite his attitude, though, he somehow re-
unites with his physical body and lives.

Later he tries to tell others, but he has trouble doing so. In
the first place, he can find no human words adequate to
describe these unearthly episodes. He also finds that others
scoff, so he stops telling other people. Still, the experience
affects his life profoundly, especially his views about death
and its relationship to life.

Do you think there is anything in Raymond Moody's work?
Could you explain what happened in any other way?
How does his account make you feel?

---

3   As an Anglican clergyman, Mark, in Margaret Craven's
story, holds Christian beliefs about life after death. Most
Christians would put their views about life and death in this
way:

> • When people die, they enter into a timeless state, like
> sleep, where time passes without them being conscious
> of it. They may, however, be conscious of feelings as
> we are when we are asleep.
> • Jesus is one day going to return to the earth. When he
> does so, there will be a resurrection. Christians who are
> in the 'sleep' of death, and who are in the 'awakeness'
> of life, will be given new bodies, similar to the one Jesus
> had when he was resurrected from the dead. (The
> stories of Easter Day, the day of Jesus' resurrection, in
> the Gospels indicate that the body of Jesus could, for
> example, pass through things.)
> • There will be a judgment of all humankind, and
> judgment will be passed according to a person's life
> and relationship to Jesus.

Read the following passages from the Bible (New
Testament) and see which verses might be used to justify
or prove such beliefs. When you have done so, re-write the

beliefs as you understand them, and after each one, list those references on which the beliefs could be based:

> Matthew chapter 25, verses 31–46
> John 14:1–3
> 1 Corinthians 15:22–24 and 35–54
> Philippians 3:20–21
> 1 Thessalonians 4:13–18

When you have done this, record your reactions to Christian belief.

---

4 Write an account of what you feel Mark might be thinking, now that he knows that the owl has called his name.

---

5 Jews and Muslims also believe, as Christians do, that after we die there is a resurrection and a judgment. The following passages from the Qur'an express Muslim belief on the subject:

The Qur'an 22.5–6

O people, if you are in doubt about the Resurrection, (consider) that We created you from dust, then of a sperm drop, then from a drop of coagulated blood, and then from a lump of flesh, formed and unformed, so that We may make things clear to you. We establish in the wombs what We will for an appointed term and then We bring you forth as infants that you may grow up and reach your prime. One dies young and another lives on to decrepitude so that he no longer knows what he used to know. You behold the earth, dry and barren, but no sooner do We send down rain upon it than it begins to stir and swell and put forth in pairs every kind of delightful growth. That is because Allah is Truth and gives life to the dead. He has power over everything. The Hour is sure to come – in this there is no doubt, and God will raise up those who are in their graves.

The Qur'an 39.67–75

They honour not Allah with the honour due to Him. And on the Day of Resurrection the entire earth will be in His grasp and the heavens will be rolled up in His right hand. Glory be to Him; exalted be He above what they associate with Him! And the trumpet shall sound and all who are in heaven and earth shall swoon, except such as Allah please. Then the trumpet will be sounded again and they shall rise and await. The earth will shine with the light of her Lord and the Book shall be set in place, and Prophets and Witnesses shall be brought and judgment will be given justly between them and they will not be wronged. And every soul will be paid back in full for what it has wrought, for God knows all its actions well. Then the unbelievers shall be driven in droves to Hell: when they draw near, its gate will then be opened to them and its keepers will say to them, 'Did there not come to you Messengers from among you who recited to you the messages of your Lord and gave you fair warning of this Day?' 'Yes indeed,' they will answer: but the decreed punishment against the unbelievers will be fulfilled and it shall be said, 'Enter the gates of Hell, to dwell therein for ever; evil is the dwelling-place of the arrogant.' But those who fear the Lord shall be led in bands to Paradise. When they draw near, its gate will be open and its keepers will say to them, 'Peace be upon you, you have been good men; enter in to dwell here for ever.' They will say, 'Praise be to God, Who has made good to us His promise and given us the earth to inherit, that we may dwell in Paradise wheresoever we please. How excellent is the reward of those who act rightly.' You shall see the Angels going round about the Throne of power proclaiming the praise of their Lord, and Judgment will be made between them fairly and it shall be said, 'Praise be to God, Lord of all worlds.'

The significant difference between this account of judgment and the way that a Christian sees it is that Christians believe they will not be punished for the wrong they have done, because Jesus (as God) was punished on their behalf when he was crucified. (See John chapter 3, verse 16; 1 Peter 2:24 and the song in chapter 53 of the Jewish book of Isaiah, which Christians believe was speaking about Jesus. See especially verse 6.)

Think through what you have learned, carefully, and write down how you react to Muslim belief.

---

6   In Eastern religion, there is a completely different understanding of life after death. James Clavell wrote a fictional story of an English sea pilot who was shipwrecked in Japan in the sixteenth century. This began many adventures, in the course of which he was taught the Japanese language by a very beautiful, married Japanese noblewoman called Mariko. They fell in love, realizing that if it became known it would mean death for them both. Their close friends saw it and discussed it:

James Clavell
Shogun

'What will happen to them, Gyoko-san?' Kiku asked softly in their palanquin on the first day of the journey.

'Disaster, Kiku-san. There's no hope for their future. He hides it well, but she . . . ! Her adoration shouts from her face. Look at her! Like a young girl! Oh, how foolish she is!'

'But oh, how beautiful, *neh*? How lucky to be so fulfilled, *neh*?'

'Yes, but even so I wouldn't wish their deaths on anyone.'

'What will Yoshinaka do when he discovers them?' Kiku asked.

'Perhaps he won't. I pray he won't. Men are such fools and so stupid. They can't see the simplest things about women, thanks be to Buddha, bless his name. Let's pray they're not discovered until we've gone about our business in Yedo. Let's pray we're not held responsible. Oh very yes! And this afternoon when we stop, let's find the nearest shrine and I'll light ten incense sticks as a god-favour. By all the gods I'll even endow a temple to all gods with three koku yearly for ten years if we escape and if I get my money.'

'But they're so beautiful together, *neh*? I've never seen a woman blossom so.'

'Yes, but she'll wither like a broken camellia when she's accused before Buntaro-san. Their *karma* is their *karma* and there's nothing we can do about them.'

In the faith of Kiku and Gyoko, the word *karma* is used almost like 'destiny'. It was believed that what happens to us in this life is determined by events in previous lives, and we cannot change things. It was believed that, when people die, they are reborn into a life shaped by lives which have already been lived.

This is very similar to Hindu belief, which is explained here by Damodar Sharma:

Damodar
Sharma and
J. Thompson
Hindu Belief
and Practice

According to the Hindu Scriptures, each individual consists of many parts: his physical body, his senses, emotions, mind, intelligence, his inner, subtle self (*jeevatma*) and his inner, spiritual self (*atma*), which may be thought of as the eternal soul. Apart from the *atma* which is supposed to be unchangeable and indestructible, all the other parts of a person are constantly being transformed. Except for the *jeevatma*, all these changing parts end when the body dies, returning to the five elements of matter: dust, liquids, heat, gases and space.

What then is a person's *jeevatma*? It is the essence of all his past experiences (probably the nearest term we have for it is 'personality'). After reading a novel, or hearing a story, or watching a television programme, we tend to forget most of the details, but remember specific parts which have impressed us in some way. Similarly some of the experiences of the life of an individual remain with him as his *jeevatma*.

When Hindus speak of reincarnation, they are referring to the *jeevatma* being reborn on earth again and again. At the end of one life, the *jeevatma* of an individual is reclothed in another physical body in its next life, and can be born as a human being, an animal, a bird, a reptile, a tree, plant, herb or any living thing. Hinduism firmly believes that the type of rebirth you get is not just a matter of chance, but is perfectly fair. It depends upon the state of your *jeevatma*, and this is shaped by your past experiences. According to the Scriptures, one suffers pain or enjoys pleasure as a result of all the deeds of your past and present lives.

6.1 Use your imagination to consider what might have happened in previous lives to bring Mariko and the Englishman together, so that they fell in love?

6.2 Write down and then discuss any evidence you have heard of which supports belief in reincarnation.

6.3 Would you say it was a pleasant prospect to face, or an unpleasant one, that a person could be reborn thousands of times?

6.4 Imagine a Christian, a Muslim and a Hindu discussing their beliefs about life after this life, and write down what they might say.

ACKNOWLEDGEMENTS

All passages from the Bible are quoted from the New International Version, copyright © 1978 by New York International Bible Society, published by Hodder and Stoughton Ltd

All passages from the Qur'an were approved by The Islamic Cultural Centre, London, England

The following extracts are included by kind permission of the copyright holders:

1 THE BEGINNINGS OF RELIGION
James Michener, extract from *The Source* reprinted by permission of the William Morris Agency

2 THE SACREDNESS OF LIFE
Nicholas Monsarrat (1951), extract from *The Cruel Sea* reprinted by permission of Mrs Ann Monsarrat
Ken Kesey, extract from *One Flew Over the Cuckoo's Nest* reprinted by permission of the publisher, Marion Boyars Publishers Ltd
Robin Cook, extract from *Brain* reprinted by permission of Deborah Rogers Ltd Literary Agency

3 CRIME AND PUNISHMENT
Laurie Lee, extract from *Cider with Rosie* reprinted by permission of the publisher, The Hogarth Press
Colleen McCullough, extract from *The Thorn Birds* reprinted by permission of the publisher, Macdonald and Co. Ltd

4 CREATION AND THE THEORY OF EVOLUTION
Irving Stone, extract from *The Origin* reprinted by permission of the publisher, Cassell Ltd

5 FAITH AND REASON
Salman Rushdie, extract from *Midnight's Children* reprinted by permission of the publisher, Jonathan Cape Ltd
Bertholt Brecht, extract from *The Life of Galileo*, translated from the German by Howard Brenton, reprinted by permission of the publisher, Methuen London

6 TO CHURCH ON SUNDAY
Flora Thompson (1945), extract from *Lark Rise to Candleford* reprinted by permission of the publisher, Oxford University Press
Peter Jenkins, *A Walk Across America* published by Lion Publishing

7 GUILT
Morris West, extract from *The Devil's Advocate* reprinted by permission of the publisher, William Heinemann Ltd
Belva Plain, extract from *Evergreen* reprinted by permission of the publisher, Collins Publishers

8 MYSTERIES OF TIME AND SPACE
Frederick Forsyth, copyright on extract from *The Shepherd* held by Frederick Forsyth 1975, reprinted by permission of Curtis Brown Ltd

9 WITCHCRAFT AND SUPERSTITION
Robert Neill, extract from *Mist Over Pendle* reprinted by permission of the publisher, Century Hutchinson Publishing Group Ltd

10 PREJUDICE
Alex Haley, extract from *Roots* reprinted by permission of the publisher, Century Hutchinson Publishing Group Ltd
Harper Lee, extract from *To Kill a Mockingbird* reprinted by permission of the publisher, William Heinemann Ltd
R. S. Thomas, 'A Welsh Testament' from *Tares* reprinted by permission of the publisher, Grafton Books, a division of The Collins Publishing Group

11 SUFFERING
Thomas Keneally, extract from *Schindler's Ark* reprinted by permission of the publisher, Hodder and Stoughton Ltd
John Godfrey Saxe, 'The Blind Men and the Elephant' from *The Book of a Thousand Poems* published by Bell and Hyman Ltd

12 DEATH AND BEYOND
Margaret Craven, extract from *I Heard the Owl Call My Name* reprinted by permission of the publisher, Harrap Ltd
Dr Raymond Moody, *Life After Life* reprinted by permission of the publisher, Bantam Books
James Clavell, extract from *Shogun* reprinted by permission of the publisher, Hodder and Stoughton Ltd
Damodar Sharma and J. Thompson, extract from *Hindu Belief and Practice* reprinted by permission of the publisher, Edward Arnold Publishers Ltd